Back to the Future

Back to the Future
Reclaiming America's Constitutional Heritage

———

James R. Evans

———

JAMESON BOOKS, INC.
OTTAWA, ILLINOIS

Jameson books are available at special discounts for bulk purchases for sales promotions, premiums, fund raising or educational use. Special condensed or excerpted paperback editions can also be created to customer specifications.

For information or other requests please write:

Jameson Books, Inc
722 Columbus Street
Ottawa, Illinois 61350
815-434-7905 • FAX 815-434-7907
E-mail 72557.3635@compuserve.com

Jameson Books titles are distributed to the book trade by LPC Group, 1436 West Randolph Street, Chicago, IL 60607. Bookstores should call 800-243-0138. Individuals who wish to order by mail should call 800-426-1357.

Library of Congress Catalog Card Number 97-075908

ISBN 0-915463-78-4

Manufactured in the United States of America
First Printing December 1997

1   2   3   4   /   99   98   97

ACKNOWLEDGMENTS

I am indebted to innumerable men and women of generations past and present for their enlightenment and encouragement.

Specifically, I want to express my appreciation and thanks to Louis Dehmlow for drawing me into the circle of those involved in the preservation of individual liberty; to Paul Harvey, who has been in the arena for so many decades, for his encouragement; to Ed Feulner, president of The Heritage Foundation, for his unequaled contributions toward a free and ordered society; to the late Leonard E. Read, past president of the Foundation for Economic Education and my most important mentor, for his guidance and wisdom; to the late Richard M. Weaver, author of the brilliant *Ideas Have Consequences,* for his encouragement; and to the late Don Lipsett, secretary of the Philadelphia Society from its inception, for his uncanny ability to hold all the intellectual elements of the conservative movement together with his "invisible hand" and for his constant help and friendship.

I want very specially to thank Dori, my partner in the world of ideas, who not only kept this project on track but also—and with good cheer—took every page of this manuscript from my word processor (which I understand and can deal with) to her computer (which I do not understand and cannot deal with), edited the pages, corrected them, added some great thoughts, and typed for hours and hours and hours.

CONTENTS

FOREWORD

Because Jim Evans and I have agreed on so many things during our long friendship, I've looked forward to the publication of this book. It has more than justified my expectations. Few contemporary American patriots have remained so consistent in their philosophical priorities.

Jim recognizes that self-government all over the world is reverting to caretaker government wherever people become complacent. He is convinced that we must learn from the lessons of history, including our own history, or risk following contemporary misleaders backward toward the Dark Ages.

Self-government won't work without self-discipline. Every ugly headline reflects this irrefutable lesson

It is difficult to get contemporaries to hear and heed admonition when Americans have never been more prosperous.

The words of Jefferson ring hollow in the ears of high school graduates who have never heard of him. Besides, the modern skeptic reasons, what could the Founding Fathers know about space ships, computers, and electronic imaging?

They couldn't. They didn't.

But modern technology won't matter if our "enlightened" generation remains ignorant about our obligation to preserve one nation under God with liberty and justice for all.

So now, let us, you and me, read this book together to see if this wonderful Republic, once worth dying for, is now worth working for.

Jim and I think it is.

PAUL HARVEY
Chicago, 1997

INTRODUCTION

T he destiny of something as rare and precious as the individual liberty and opportunity bestowed upon the citizens of the United States of America by the founding fathers ought not to be lightly regarded or taken for granted. Unfortunately, ample evidence suggests that we may have done just that—that we may, indeed, have shrugged away our birthright.

Although the growth of centralized government and the loss of individual liberty have been major concerns throughout the twentieth century, the acceleration of that trend over the past thirty-five years warrants serious consideration. Historically, when governments intrude upon the personal lives of their citizens, when they undermine religious absolutes, when they substitute social engineering for personal responsibility, civilizations decline both morally and economically. There have been no exceptions.

Is it possible that Americans have come to prefer poverty and immorality to the freedom and virtue that create prosperity and civil behavior?

I admit to a strong and lifelong preference for: limited government, a free market based on willing exchange, the sanctity of private property, and the restoration of traditional values. Anyone who values a "free and ordered society" must face the fact that, by any set of reasonable measurements, our individual freedom has diminished considerably and we are besieged by rampant disorder.

As I hope this book will establish, our nation will face the tragedy of bankruptcy unless there is a change in thinking which leads to a change in behavior.

We have abandoned our own Revolution, our Declaration of Independence, our Constitution, and our Bill of Rights by subscribing to a program of high taxes, deficit spending, and inflationary measures. The signposts of history designate this as a downhill route.

This is not, however, an economic treatise or a political platform. It is a book about ideas. In particular, it is a reexamination of the unique ideas upon which this nation was conceived—ideas about man, God, and government. If those ideas seem to be unappreciated by many among our media elite, our academic communities, and our citizenry at large, I think it is because they possess little or no understanding of the ideas themselves or of the fact that they are the foundation of human liberty.

Richard M. Weaver, in his masterful *Ideas Have Consequences*, establishes that unshakable premise, using America as his most significant example.

Ideas are conclusions reached through conscious or subconscious reasoning, and logical reasoning is based on premises. Conclusions—whether they are reached deductively or inductively—will be unsound unless their basic premises are solid and certain.

People will, however, often accept premises that only *appear* reasonable or that are widely accepted. In such cases, the conclusions they draw are likely to be vague and overgeneralized, if not downright contradictory to fact. Those flawed conclusions, in turn, become questionable premises, and so on until a structure has been erected that looks impressive but will collapse under the slightest pressure.

It is extremely dangerous to live in such a structure.

Consider for a moment the *blitzkrieg* of premises—some facts, some opinions expressed as if they were facts—which bombard us almost every hour of every day. Newspapers, television, magazines, radio, books, and personal contacts strafe us with information, and in the barrage fact merges with opinion and melts into mass-produced confusion.

How often has a newspaper editorial, a magazine article, or a television commentary begun with, "As all Americans know ..." or "In view of the fact that ..." or "It is common knowledge that ..."? These preludes set the stage for opinions-expressed-as-facts that may or may not be valid. If there is no valid premise, we may be swallowing misleading clichés or getting a dose of intellectual contamination that will pollute our thinking over time. When this condition affects a large part of our population, our survival as free individuals is in extreme jeopardy.

Ideas *do* have consequences. Words *do* matter. Our birthright of individual liberty is the offshoot of ideas, and so is the threat to its survival.

Many Americans seem to have accepted the ideas that have permeated our politics for the past four decades without questioning their validity. This book is for them. Others have no identifiable political philosophy, and this book is also for them. The increasing burden the state places on our lives and the lives of our children demands serious attention. It is our responsibility, our duty, to participate in the determination of our own futures and those of our children.

Many of us, regardless of our differences, possess deep, heartfelt beliefs about the relationship between man and government. Unfortunately, in spite of the strength of our convictions, we may have trouble defending those beliefs. This book attempts to clarify and restate political principles in a way that I hope will add ammunition to our arsenal in this argument.

Clearly, then, this book was not intended as an exposé, but that is what portions of it have become. Any search for truth leads where it leads, and in this case it has led to a discussion of the consequences of sacrificing values to political expediency.

Who will speak openly against individual liberty? No one. But there are many who propose, support, or simply accept scheme after scheme that limits liberty, raises taxes, grants the state increased power over our lives, and/or trades opportunity for the "security" of government control.

Does personal freedom depend on economic freedom? Unequivocally, yes. Can economic growth occur in the absence of economic freedom? Absolutely not. These are the lessons of both history and current events.

In an effort to fill a void in the knowledge needed by those who choose to live in a free and ordered society, this book will discuss:

- What the vast majority of Americans, through no fault of their own, simply don't know—and why they don't know it.

- What an even larger percentage of Americans, again through no fault of their down, "know" that simply isn't so—and how they "know" it.

- The ideas that led our founding fathers to create the most profound documents dedicated to liberty ever conceived, and the sources from which those ideas were derived—i.e., what the founders intended to do and why they wanted to do it.

- The basic foundations of a free and ordered society.

- What the government of the United States is, how it functions, what it is supposed to do, and what it is not supposed to do.

- The true nature of the American business community and the economy it supports—i.e., how business functions and what it provides.

- The last three decades of government activism and their logical consequences.

- Political labels—liberal, conservative, left, right, extreme, and moderate—and how they affect today's politics.

Without a thorough understanding of the unique beginnings of our nation, it is simply not possible intelligently to assess what now emanates from the three branches of our federal government.

The information here has been thoroughly researched and is both accurate and documented. Some of the ideas and opinions contained here are controversial; others are "for motherhood and against sin."

Principles presented here, and their applications, are timeless. References to activities of recent or current administrations and Congresses in Chapters 1 and 12 are intended only to fortify my contentions about the dangers that can beset an ill-informed or misinformed electorate.

It is not my intent to "change anyone's mind." My purpose is to provide the other half of the equation, the half that our system of public education has neglected—to give what Paul Harvey calls "The Rest of the Story."

Thomas Jefferson once wrote, "If a Nation, in a state of civilization, expects to be ignorant and free, it expects what never was and never will be." It is to the restoration of learning and liberty that this book is dedicated.

CHAPTER ONE

The American Condition

Political history will, I believe, record that for the past forty years the two major political parties have more often functioned as one party than as two. True, Democrats controlled both houses of Congress almost exclusively for sixty years, until 1994, and that control did result in an ever-increasing number of federal programs with the predictable upward spiral in expenditures, taxes, and public debt. Nevertheless, the Republican reaction to this increasing governmental activity was largely rhetorical.

It took 175 years from the founding of the Republic to bring the annual cost of the federal government to a hundred billion dollars in 1962. *It then took only 33 years of profligate spending to raise the cost by fifteen times—an increase 375 times that of our population growth!*[1]

It can be argued that the American people apparently approved this spending binge, because they returned control of the Congress to the same political party in election after election, no matter which party won the White House. And since the Congress controls spending, it could be reasonably assumed that there were no substantial popular objections—until recently.

I use the word *apparently* for a reason: Over that thirty-three-year period, the average election was decided by less than 34 percent of the eligible voters (approximately 20 percent of the population). What the media reports as "51 percent of the American people" actually translates to 20 percent of the population. But *why* is voter turnout so low?[2] Why would a supposedly knowledgeable citizenry act in such a fashion? Why—given this spendthrift government—does the economy *appear* reasonably stable?

And, most important, why are the citizens of the United States not experiencing euphoric feelings of relief and well-being?

The Soviet Union has collapsed from a centralized menace into a group of quarreling entities, thus considerably reducing our risk of nuclear obliteration. Most of the ugly political ideas that have threatened the Republic—fascism, communism, and other nutcake-isms—have been relegated to the lunatic fringe. Our standard of living has risen to a point undreamt of only a few generations ago. Our former luxuries have become absolute necessities. Even those designated "poor" by government standards live amid what our grandparents would have considered luxuries, in conditions equal to or better than those deemed "middle-class" in other industrial societies.

For some reason, though, expressions of euphoria—or even satisfaction—are rare. Americans, we are told, are angry, perplexed, frustrated, confused, uncertain, and dreadfully fearful of the future. In other words, there is a lot of "whining" going on out there.

Is the whining justified? The answer is a resounding and obvious "No!" Are the assorted feelings of anger, perplexity, frustration, confusion, uncertainty, and fear of the future understandable? My unqualified answer is, "Yes!"

November 1994

These various discontents were expressed politically in November of 1994 when the Republican party swept the off-year congressional elections and took control of both houses for the first time in forty years. Political pundits were totally astounded. Not a single incumbent Republican congressman, senator, or governor was defeated. For the first time in more than twenty years, Republicans won a majority of the nation's governorships and control of seventeen state legislatures. But it was the methodology that really stunned the political pundits.

Sensing public resentment of an arrogant Democratic Congress basking confidently in forty years of power over the nation's wallet, a group of conservative Republicans crafted the Contract with America, subtitled "Promises Made/ Promises Kept." They intended, they said, to bring fundamental change to the House of Representatives. On September 27, 1994, the document was unveiled and signed by 367 candidates—both incumbents and challengers.

The signers agreed on five principles:

1. Individual liberty
2. Economic opportunity
3. Limited government
4. Personal responsibility
5. Security at home and abroad

The Contract promised that, given a new Republican majority, legislators would pass *on the first day of the 104th Congress* the following major reforms aimed at restoring the faith and trust of the American people in their government:

1. They would require all laws that apply to the rest of the country to apply equally to the Congress.
2. They would engage a major independent auditing firm to conduct a comprehensive audit of the Congress for waste, fraud, and abuse.
3. They would cut the number of House committees and the size of committee staffs by one third.
4. They would impose term limits on all committee chairs. They would ban the casting of proxy votes in

committee. They would require that committee meetings be open to the public.

5. They would require a three-fifths majority vote to pass a tax increase.
6. They would guarantee an honest accounting of the federal budget by implementing zero baseline budgeting.

They further vowed that in the first one hundred days of the 104th Congress, they would bring to the House floor ten key bills, each of which would be given full and open debate, and a clear and fair vote; and each of which would be available that same day for public scrutiny.

During the ensuing campaign the administration scoffed, political experts sneered, and the media laughed derisively. The consensus was that such promises were ludicrous, and that the entire "gimmicky" idea would backfire.

On November 8, 1994, the laughter ceased abruptly. An upset of such magnitude astounded both the media in general and the political prognosticators in particular. The real significance of the event, however, was the hope it offered that a true two-party system might reemerge for the first time in four decades. Could a genuine two-party Congress actually debate the issues surrounding the proper role of government? Could the positions of the proponents and opponents of a given issue become clearly defined?

As the post-election shock wore off, the citizenry went "out to lunch"—that is, its attention wandered. On the first day of the opening session of the new 104th Congress, the House of Representatives *actually passed every reform it had promised!* During the next ninety-three days, the House fulfilled the Contract by bringing all ten bills to the floor for debate and vote. (Term limitation was filibustered, primarily by the Democrats, and didn't come to a vote.) For the first time in memory legislative promises were made and kept, but the net effect was to move "ten miles of arrogant power-grabbing over a thirty-year span back one mile"—hardly a radical change.

Reaction to the Contract

Instead of enthusiastic applause from the electorate and rave reviews from the media, this performance was met with a resounding yawn or with cries of righteous indignation: "You can't do that! It's too extreme!"

Clearly, the vast majority of the American public had no real understanding of the substance of the legislation, which was directed toward reducing the size, scope, and cost of the federal government by re-establishing the force of Amendment X of the Constitution:

> *The powers not delegated to the United States by the Constitution, nor prohibited by it to the States, are reserved to the States respectively, or to the people.*

Why *didn't* the electorate understand the significance of this legislation? In this instance, the American people cannot be entirely faulted for their lack of knowledge. Understanding why they are not at fault—and who is—is the key to understanding the American Condition.

Consider: If you had never studied mathematics or even simple arithmetic, if therefore you could not add, subtract, multiply, or divide—much less find the value of X—could you balance your checkbook? calculate your taxes? Without some basic science classes, would you know the danger of oily rags meeting lighted matches?

Well, then—what if you've received little or no instruction about the sources and intent of our Declaration of Independence, our Constitution, or our Federalist Papers? What if you know virtually nothing of the history of this continent between the landing of the first pilgrims and the final deliberations, 170 years later, out of which these fundamental documents evolved? What if you are unaware of the principles and traditions on which our liberty was founded? How prepared will you be to judge wisely the recent history of our government or the merits of current legislation?

In fact, the vast majority of Americans have never been given this vital educational exposure.

Noah Webster said, "God grants liberty only to those who love it and are willing to fight for it." If that is so, then to whom do we owe gratitude for our blessings of liberty and opportunity? Most people would agree that we owe our thanks to those courageous men and women who first touched our shores in 1607 and to the colonists who followed them during the next 182 years. They not only placed their very survival on the line in exchange for the mere possibility of freedom, but also encapsulated the very essence of liberty in the Declaration of Independence and its companion, the Constitution of the United States. In the process, they fought the Revolutionary War against well-trained, well-armed, well-paid British redcoats—and won. (We are, of course, equally indebted to every American who has taken up arms in defense of our freedom over the last two centuries.) History clearly validates the ominous warning of Thomas Philpot Kern: "Vigilance is the price of liberty."

The Lessons of History

If you believe that "History repeats itself," consider the great historian Edward Gibbon's *The Decline and Fall of the Roman Empire*. Gibbon sets forth the five basic reasons why that great civilization withered and died:

1. The dignity and sanctity of the home, which is the basic unit of human society, were undermined.
2. The government demanded higher and higher taxes, and spent public money for free bread and circuses for the populace.
3. The population became more and more devoted to the pursuit of pleasure.
4. Armaments were provided for the military in spite of the fact that the real enemy—the decay of individual responsibility—was within Rome itself.

5. Religion decayed, and faith faded into mere form, losing touch with real life and thereby losing its power to guide the people.

Or as the conventional wisdom used to tell us, the average age of the world's great civilizations has been two hundred years. These nations went through the following sequence:

From bondage to spiritual faith.
From spiritual faith to great courage.
From courage to liberty.
From liberty to abundance.
From abundance to selfishness.
From selfishness to complacency.
From complacency to apathy.
From apathy to dependence.
From dependence back to bondage.

If we give any credence to these and other lessons of history, it becomes difficult to ignore the considerable evidence that over the past half century our freedoms have been declining at an increasing rate, and that our relationship to our government is changing in ways the founders would not have countenanced.

It is necessary for us to confront the troubling contradictions of our time: This land of liberty, founded on the principles of individual liberty and civil behavior, has out-produced the entire world within less than two centuries of its birth; it has become the greatest economic and military power in history; it has provided the highest standard of living ever known. But it has also become the biggest debtor nation in the industrialized world; engendered the highest rate of violent crime in the industrialized world; recorded the highest rate of teenage and unmarried pregnancies in the industrialized world; tripled—over the last thirty-five years—the constant dollars spent per public school student, while watching students' SAT scores tumble to a level second to last among industrialized nations; and seen teenage drug use rise by 78 percent in the past four years, and cocaine use by 105 percent in the past two years.[3]

These perplexing inconsistencies, coupled with the nature of recent political rhetoric, certainly contribute to the confusion and uncertainty expressed by many Americans.

The simple truth is that you can fool *most* of the people *most* of the time—*if* they lack knowledge or understanding of the principles that underlie their freedom. If we have not been thoroughly schooled in the history of our founding documents—the sources from which the principles were drawn—and the intent of those who created them, we become easy targets for sophistry and dissembling.

Why We Don't Know

"Is it possible to evaluate with wisdom anything of which we have limited knowledge"?

I asked myself that very question many years ago after I'd completed my formal education and realized just how limited my knowledge was. I could identify historical documents, and I knew a little colonial history, but that was it. It was only by a fluke that I stumbled into more than forty years of research and study of the subject.

A few years ago, watching with amazement some of the goings-on in all three branches of our federal government and at the same time reading about the history of our educational system, I realized two things that stunned me:

1. If, having attended highly regarded public schools and the University of Michigan, I had received almost no education about the roots of our unique heritage, the history of the colonial experience, the creation of the Declaration of Independence, the Constitution, the Bill of Rights, and the Federalist Papers, much less the

sources from which they were drawn—then how many people born after 1920 had learned as much or more? Obviously, our public school system had simply not seen fit to devote more than passing attention to the subject since the mid-1930s.

2. I had supposed—logically, it seemed to me—that anyone with a law degree would be well versed in American history. How else could an attorney deal with constitutional interpretation? But I was wrong. Interviews with more than twenty highly successful practicing attorneys of all ages—graduates of prestigious law schools including Yale, Harvard, Michigan, and the University of Chicago—revealed unanimously that there were *no* required courses in such history or philosophy, and only a few students took advantage of the electives offered in those areas of study. Their concentration was on "case law."

Do we conclude, then, that the general population—including the media and the members of the legal profession (who, among other things, staff our governmental institutions)—lacks adequate knowledge of the historical background, the causes, the philosophy, the intent or content, and even the authors of our founding documents? Indeed.

All these ingredients contribute to the American Condition. We know, on a "gut" level, that we observe a lack of common sense in government, that things are not quite what they should be. But we are ill-equipped to evaluate the reasons.

So the fundamental question becomes, Why do we lack this knowledge?

Consider the sources from which we receive our information.

The advent of mass communications was, in a great many respects, a boon to humanity. When radio was born, the dissemination of news was only one aspect of broadcasting—and not the major one. True, the radio carried election news in 1920 and brought Franklin Roosevelt to the nation's firesides in the 1930s. But radio was largely an entertainment medium, described by some as the successor to vaudeville. Newscasts aired at noon and in the evening and lasted only fifteen minutes. When World War II broke out, radio news became more important, and some newsmen (e.g., Edward R. Murrow, William Shirer) became celebrities. Nevertheless, people continued to rely for the full story on newspapers and newsmagazines. Television was able to combine the immediacy of a human voice with the vividness of a photograph. TV began with fifteen-minute newscasts, but quickly lengthened them. The faces of the newscasters became as familiar as those of movie stars—and were brought into homes through the same medium.

The Information Glut

The information age was upon us. Reuters, UPI, and others fed all media outlets. Journalism students began to envision themselves as "investigative reporters" à la Woodward and Bernstein. The percentage of television time devoted to news exploded. Newspapers began to go out of business because so many people were relying on broadcast news—and reliance on broadcast news increased as a result of this dearth of newspapers. Reporters evolved into news analysts, and twenty-four-hour-a-day news stations proliferated on both radio and television. Cable television hit the ground running, gave birth to CNN, and inundated us with information.

Now the marvels of the computer age and the miracles of electronic communications have given a relatively small segment of our society the influence of a "fourth branch of government," a branch at least as influential as the three others.

Like anyone who acquires excess power, many members of the media have adopted an air of arrogance, dispensing editorial opinions as though they were facts, committing journalistic sins of omission, and blurring the once-sacrosanct borders between news, features, and editorials.

They thrive on conflict, which attracts audiences and must therefore be created where it does not exist. Where there is complexity, these media personages simplify and explain, not trusting viewers and listeners to form their own impressions and opinions.

A thorough survey of the major media following the 1992 election revealed that 91 percent of its members voted exclusively for Democratic candidates. Some 71 percent classified themselves as liberal, and 7 percent as conservative. If you are skeptical of statistics, consider this: On March 21, 1996, at the Radio and TV Correspondents Association Dinner, *eminence grise* Walter Cronkite remarked, "Everybody knows that there's a heavy liberal persuasion among correspondents." And Evan Thomas of *Newsweek*—hardly a conservative—stated, "There is a liberal bias. It's demonstrable. About 85 percent of the reporters who cover the White House vote Democratic—they have for a long time. There is particularly at the networks' lower levels, among editors and the so-called infrastructure, a liberal bias."

In all fairness, total objectivity is difficult to achieve, and the reporters themselves are not entirely responsible for their disproportionate influence.

The Medium and the Message

The assassination of John F. Kennedy had a far greater immediate impact on the world than did the crucifixion of Christ, simply because most of the world learned of J.F.K.'s assassination within twenty minutes of its occurrence. The effect of almost instantaneous universal knowledge is dramatically magnified shock. And the faces and voices that transmit this information assume almost mythic significance.

Of course, everyone is entitled to a personal viewpoint. On the other hand, the power the media bestow on the purveyors of news carries with it the responsibility to aim for reasonable objectivity. When this responsibility is denied or ignored, when the news is delivered with condescending "explanations" (often based on incorrect premises, misleading data, and disdain for traditional values), the public reacts with understandable anger.

As a reaction to such practices, radio and television talk shows (both credible and suspect) have multiplied like rabbits, and C-SPAN has sprung up to offer balanced, undiluted reporting, and an arena for open and public debate. But in spite of these new options, the prime-time elite continue to dominate for the moment. And they must share the blame for the things we know that are not so.

Do they contribute to our uncertainty and our fear of the future? Yes, but so do several other factors. For instance, in fiscal year 1962, American taxpayers were "charged" $274 million a day in federal taxes. By 1994, that figure had skyrocketed to $4.1 billion a day—a fifteen-fold increase. When state and local taxes are added, the average American worker pays more than 40 percent of his or her earnings in taxes every year. (If you add an estimated $6,000 in regulatory costs per family per year, the rate rises to 50 percent or more.)[4] The word for that is *confiscatory*. At the current (1995) rate of deficit growth, in the year 2000, 85 percent of total projected personal and corporate income tax receipts will be required to pay only the *interest* on the debt. Imagine using 85 percent of your paycheck to pay the monthly interest on your credit card debt, leaving only 15 percent for all other expenses—including the credit card debt itself.)[5]

I suggest, therefore, that anyone who *isn't* angry, perplexed, frustrated, confused, uncertain, and dreadfully fearful of the future simply hasn't been paying attention.

The question of where and how we as a people derive our rights underlies the current political struggle and, indeed, every political issue that confronts us.

That is why this book is being written—in an effort to condense the knowledge necessary for anyone who hopes to understand and evaluate the state of our nation and to measure the efficacy of proposed or existing legislation. The bibliography lists the references from which this information has been drawn.

We begin with our founding fathers in their search for a free and ordered society.

Notes

1. *Statistical Abstract of the United States, 1993* (Washington, D.C.: Government Printing Office, 1994).
2. Ibid.
3. William J. Bennett, *Index of Leading Cultural Indicators: Facts and Figures on the State of American Society* (New York: Simon & Schuster, 1994).
4. Martin Gross, *A Call for Revolution* (New York: Ballantine, 1993).
5. Harry E. Figgie Jr. and Gerald J. Swanson, *Bankruptcy 1995* (Boston: Little, Brown, 1992).

CHAPTER TWO

The Path to the Declaration

The Declaration of Independence was, in a very real sense, the blueprint for the Constitution. Literally all of the philosophical elements of true human liberty are embodied in the Declaration itself. The Constitution, though lengthier and considerably more complex, simply set up the governmental framework required to implement and protect the natural rights expressed in the Declaration.

The founders, having reached agreement on the liberties to which free men and women are entitled, then reassembled to establish the institutions and methodology that would prevent a government from becoming—like governments throughout history—a tyranny.

It was an unprecedented challenge, a challenge not met by the brilliant democracy of Greece, the robust republic of Rome, or the determined English lords who forced their king to sign the Magna Carta.

The founders met that challenge. Unlike the Constitution, which was deliberately constructed as an amendable document, the Declaration was accepted as a factual statement of immutable truth.

Almost 170 years passed between the founding of Jamestown, Virginia, in 1607 and the signing of the Declaration of Independence on July 4, 1776. During those years, thousands of settlers seeking religious, civil, and/or personal liberty abandoned homes and families and risked their lives to cross an enormous expanse of ocean. They thought of themselves as colonists, subjects of the King of England, but together they created an environment in which thirteen separate colonies could join forces in a united effort to seize their independence from that king and that country.

In 1620—early in this period of immigration and settlement—the Pilgrim fathers drafted the Mayflower Compact, setting out fundamental agreements by which they would live in the Plymouth Colony of Massachusetts. Only nineteen years later another group of colonists composed the Fundamental Orders of Connecticut. These documents rejected the divine right of kings—the idea that kings were chosen by God to rule over other men and could determine what rights their subjects would and would not have. The colonists asserted that the source of man's rights was the Creator, not the King, and that government must be based on the contractual consent of the governed.

It should, therefore, have been expected that the actions of the British Parliament—regarding, for example, taxation of the colonists and the housing of the King's troops—would be met with protests. The refusal by the King, his ministers, and his Parliament to acknowledge the rights of the colonists led to the convening of the First Continental Congress in Philadelphia in September 1774. There they produced a list of their grievances against King George III, and within six months the opening shots of the Revolutionary War were fired at Lexington and Concord. The final spark was set off by the publication of Thomas Paine's pamphlet *Common Sense* in January of 1776. Paine's words generated a massive increase in public support for a break with England.

On June 7, 1776, Richard Henry Lee of Virginia placed the following resolution before the Continental Congress:

That these United States are, and of right ought to be, free and Independent States, that they are absolved from all allegiance to the British Crown, and that all political connections between them and the State of Great Britain is, and ought to be, totally dissolved.

The committee appointed to draw up the Declaration of Independence consisted of John Adams, Benjamin Franklin, Roger Sherman, and Robert J. Livingston, with Thomas Jefferson as chairman. Although all of them contributed, the final draft was primarily Jefferson's work.

The sources of the principles embodied in the Declaration were many and varied. The authors drew from the Ten Commandments, the teachings of Christ, the ideals of John Calvin and Martin Luther, and the Magna Carta. From John Locke's *Treatises on Government* came clarification of the meaning of "endowed rights"; from Sir William Blackstone's *Commentaries*, the perceptions of justice and of the inseparability of human and property rights; from the Pilgrims, the reflections on their experiences expressed in the Petition of Rights and the Mayflower Compact.

A glance at the diary of Governor William Bradford of the Plymouth Colony provides interesting insights into the "pilgrims' progress." Most history books neglect to mention that the pilgrims at first established a communal economic system—a very simple form of communism. All settlers were to produce according to their ability and contribute their production to a common storehouse from which they could draw according to their needs. Human nature, however, was then as it is now, and in a short time the pilgrims found themselves on the edge of starvation. According to Governor Bradford's account, he and his advisors called the colonists together and suggested that a new system be implemented. From then on, each settler could do as he chose with the results of his labor:

This had a very good success; for it made all hands very industrious, so much as more corne was planted than other waise would have bene by means of gov. or any other could use, and saved him a great deall of trouble, and give farr better contente. The women now wente willingly into the field, and tooke their little-on's with them to set corne, which before would aledg weakness, and inabilitie; whom to have compelled would have bene thought tiranie and oppression. . . . By this time harvest was come, and instead of famine, now God gave them plentie, and the face of things was changed, to the rejoysing of the harts of many, for which they blessed God . . . and some of the abler sort and more industrious had to spare, and sell to others, so as any generll wante or famine hath not been amongest them since to this day.

In a sense, the American spirit was born of that decision, and from it came the flame that would ignite the American Revolution more than a century and a half later.

And what about the American pioneers who followed? Certainly, most were not intellectuals—they had not studied philosophy or political science. But they had lived with, and therefore understood, tyranny and regimentation—and they wanted none of it.

There was little that government could do for them. It couldn't clear land for farming or build a cabin. So they acknowledged that the source of their great gifts of life, liberty, and property was neither a man nor a government. With the intense love of individual liberty that belongs to those who have experienced tyranny, they grasped the simple proposition that their personal liberty and freedom of choice rested almost entirely on their willingness to assume personal responsibility and seek its counterpart—opportunity.

Paul Harvey describes the pioneer experience this way:

... in but a few years, free men raised themselves and their society to a pinnacle of progress unapproached in all the ages. When America's early pioneers first turned their eyes toward the West, they did not demand that somebody take care of them when they got ill or old. They did not demand maximum pay for no work at all. Come to think of it, they did not demand much of anything—except freedom.

They looked out at those rolling plains stretching away to the tall, green mountains, then lifted their eyes to the blue skies and said, "Thank you, God. I can take it from here."

This nation was not carved out of the wilderness, as some say. It was scratched and chopped and dug and hammered and clawed out. No government ever gave to its citizens what hardworking Americans with their sleeves rolled up have earned for themselves. Our citizens stood on their own two feet and asked nothing for nothing and elected leaders to match. There was poverty, but there was opportunity. There were hardships, but there was hope. There was security.

Here, at last, was the security men had sought for six thousand years. A land in which a man was entitled to all the prerogatives of a man. He could climb as high as he could carry his own weight. Because he got wherever he was under his own steam, he was secure. Some failed and failed to rise again. So there were poorhouses, as well as mansions. That was the important part. The fact that here the only things which prevent the man in the poorhouse from living in a mansion were his own limitations.[1]

The Declaration was actually constructed in two parts. The second, and much longer, portion was essentially a catalog of grievances listing twenty-seven specific abuses perpetrated by the British. They ranged from *"He had erected a multitude of new Offices, and sent hither swarms of Officers to harass our People, and eat out their substance"* to *"For imposing taxes upon us without our consent."* (NB: Some things never change.

) The second paragraph of the first part sets out the basic premise that separates the American experiment in the man-government relationship from all others:

> *We hold these truths to be self-evident, that all men are created equal, that they are endowed by their Creator with certain unalienable Rights, that among them are Life, Liberty, and the pursuit of Happiness. That to secure these rights, Governments are instituted among Men, deriving their just powers from the consent of the governed. That whenever any Form of Government becomes destructive of these ends, it is the right of the people to alter or to abolish it.*

The notion that *"all men are created equal"* is somewhat ambiguous. Clearly, Jefferson was not suggesting that all men are identical in talent, character, achievement, etc., and none of the authors endorsed the idea of government-imposed equality. "All human beings are equal in the eyes of God and under the law" states the case, as does the Virginia Declaration of Rights: "All men are by nature equally free and independent."

John Adams and the other founders knew that the equality of human beings did not do away with degrees of merit and virtue. But they believed that the elimination of the class system—no more earls, no more dukes, no more barons—would offer, for the first time in history, a genuine opportunity for everyone, regardless of his or her birth, to be rewarded for true virtue and merit.

The truly unprecedented concept set forth in the Declaration of Independence is this: The source of man's rights is not a king, a state, or a parliament. The source of man's rights is not other men—not even a majority of other men. No—instead, men.... *"are endowed by their Creator with certain unalienable rights; that among these are life, liberty and the pursuit of happiness ..."* And government is forbidden to infringe on or violate these God-given rights.

In his classic essay, "Endowed by Their Creator," the late Leonard E. Read writes:

> The full implication of the phrase "endowed by their Creator with certain unalienable rights; that among these are life, liberty, and the pursuit of happiness" is, quite obviously, a political concept with tremendous spiritual overtones. Indeed, this concept is at once spiritual, political and economic. It is spiritual in proclaiming the Creator as the endower of men's rights and, thus, a sovereign. It is political in the sense that such an acknowledgment implicitly denies the State as the endower of men's rights and, thus, the State is not sovereign. And this is an economic concept because it follows from a man's inherent right to life that he has the right to sustain his life, the sustenance of life being nothing more or less than the fruits of one's own labor.
>
> ... Unless we believe that man's rights are an endowment of our Creator and, therefore, unalienable, we must conclude that the rights to life and liberty derive from some human collective and that they are alienable, being at the disposal of the collective will. There is no third alternative: *we believe in one or we submit to the other.* If the latter, there is no freedom in the social sense; there is despotism.
>
> If we lack this spiritual faith, our rights to life and liberty are placed on the altar of collective caprice and they must suffer whatever fate the political apparatus dictates.
>
> If the concept regarding the source of our rights is as expressed in our Declaration of Independence then Government, logically, can have no powers beyond those which individuals may properly exercise.[2]

In this context it is important to distinguish between *freedom to* and *freedom from.* If our basic idea of freedom is sound in premise and consistent in logic, then our freedoms are freedoms *to:* Freedom for each individual to utilize and expand his Creator-given rights to life, liberty, and the pursuit of happiness is the touchstone of our liberty.

Freedom *from* is well represented in Articles 118 through 122 of the original Soviet Constitution. Every right you can imagine is listed, but—those rights come from and are controlled by the state. And so they are not "rights" at all.

A classic example of "freedom from" is found in Starr Daily's private journal entitled *Through Valleys to Victory*. He is, he attests, free from hunger, free from the lack of inadequate clothing, free from unemployment, free from lack of medical care, free from the fear of insecurity in his old age, and free from economic crisis. Of course, when he wrote this journal, Daily was an inmate in a prison hospital! Loaded with freedom from, but utterly regimented and therefore devoid of freedom to.

It is also significant that our founders were men of means who stood to lose everything—money, land, influence—by rebelling. They were well educated. Twenty four were lawyers and judges. Eleven were merchants of one variety or another, and nine were farmers and plantation owners. All of them could have accepted the British yoke and continued to lead comfortable lives. Yet they were willing to trade their security and well-being to midwife an embryonic nation at best, or hang from a rope at worst.

They mutually pledged their lives, their fortunes and their sacred honor, and many paid a heavy price. Nine were reduced to poverty within a very short time. Five were captured by the British, imprisoned, and died within a few years. Twelve had their homes, farms, or plantation sacked, looted, or burned by the British. Nine died during the war.

They pledged—and they paid—and they delivered our freedom.[3] The lesson they left us is this:

We cannot separate our spiritual from our economic or political ideas and remain free, for in a spiritual vacuum personal discipline collapses, and tyranny will inevitably fill the void.

The final draft of the Declaration of Independence was adopted on July 4, 1776. (The actual signing did not take place until August 2, 1776.)*

While the Declaration of Independence was being drafted, the Articles of Confederation were written to unite the colonies. What John Dickinson and his committee produced, however, amounted to little more than a league of friendship. It was certainly not the basis for a national government. For that, we would need the Constitution.

Notes
1. Paul Harvey, *Remember These Things* (Chicago: Heritage Press, 1952).
2. Leonard E. Read, *Essays on Liberty,* (Irvington-on-Hudson, N.Y.: Foundation for Economic Education, 1962).
3. Harvey, *Remember.*

*For your reference, the Declaration of Independence is reprinted in Appendix A.

CHAPTER THREE

The Constitution

Even with the Declaration of Independence as a blueprint, drafting a constitution was a herculean task for the founders. A decade of turmoil and deadlock followed the Revolutionary War.

Fresh from their struggle to escape English domination, Americans were in no mood to create another strong central government. Each colony attempted to produce its own version of a constitution, but the determination of each state to be independent repeatedly ran headlong into the obvious need for unity.

Fortunately, the men who assembled in Philadelphia in May of 1787 were an extraordinary lot. All of them were familiar with what we now call the Judaeo-Christian ethic. Most of them had studied both Latin and Greek, and had read the works of the great classical historians: Herodotus, Plato, Aristotle, Cicero, Livy, and Plutarch. They knew about earlier experiments in democracy and were aware of the various reasons that each had collapsed. Their knowledge of the structure and functions of the British Parliament was thorough. Many were also familiar with the writings of the French philosophers Rousseau, Condorcet, and Turgot the men who planted the seeds of the coming French Revolution. These sources and many others combined with the colonial experience itself to create what John Adams referred to as the "lamp of experience," which would be their guide. Let's briefly consider what knowledge and beliefs they brought with them to that meeting room.

The Ten Commandments Moses delivered to the Israelites posited man as self-controlling—i.e., responsible for his own thoughts, words, and actions. Most important, this code of conduct acknowledged that man receives his rights from God the Creator, not from other men and not from any government. Belief in God, however, is not necessary for acceptance or understanding of that point. On a purely natural level, it is clear that man was here first—before any government existed—so human life and human rights cannot depend on a government. Life, of course, presupposes the right to sustain life, the right of human beings to maintain and improve their lot. That right is also inherent, and not the gift of a government.

The Judaic law is unequivocal on property rights as well: "Thou shall not steal." The right to hold private property, honestly acquired, is essential to human freedom. Without it, you are free to take my property at will and by force if you can. And vice versa. The brilliant French political scientist Frederic Bastiat stated the proposition with devastating clarity:

> Life, liberty and property do not exist because men have made laws. On the contrary, it was the fact that life, liberty, and property existed beforehand that caused men to make laws in the first place.[1]

To judge the merit of an idea that involves the relationship between man and government, our first question must be: Does this idea encourage or discourage the utilization of free, creative human energy?

Some ancient laws served the convention delegates by illustrating what a government should *not* do. The ancient Code of Hammurabi, for example, imposed rigid controls on wages, prices, production, and consumption. Personal freedom and economic freedom were both sacrificed to the will of the government.

In the fourth century BC, the people of Athens allowed their rulers to usurp certain of their freedoms. Grain inspectors and other government agents scrutinized and regulated production of all kinds, weakening both the society and the very government that had imposed the new system.

The delegates sent to the Constitutional Convention by the thirteen states knew these and many more lessons of history, and were dedicated to protecting their fledgling nation from avoidable errors. They deliberated in closed session, seeking some equilibrium between the powers of the states and those of the federal government. They intended to spell out very clearly the limitations of federal authority and, at the same time, to erect barriers against the mob rule which had plagued earlier democracies. They also strove to incorporate what they had learned from their recent experience with the British Parliament and from the American colonies themselves.

The need for the separation of powers among a bicameral legislature, an executive branch, and a judicial branch was obvious, and its adoption required only limited debate. But structuring a viable system of checks and balances (to prevent any given branch from acquiring excess power) proved contentious. The judiciary would be largely—though not entirely—independent of the two other branches. By staggering lengths of terms and providing for a presidential veto, the delegates sought to restrain any factions that would seek radical or ill-considered change. The system of elections and impeachment procedures, would, they hoped, foster responsible and responsive government. This constitution would be the law of the land and would apply primarily not to private individuals, but to government itself.[2]

The specific provisions of the Constitution limited government by defining and distributing its powers. Power was divided vertically among national, state, and local governments. This is the meaning of *federalism*. The system of overlapping functions and of checks and balances divided power horizontally at the national level.

From late May until September 17, 1787, the delegates debated the constitution's structure, articles, and—most important—intent. Although most delegates made contributions, the giants of the convention were Ben Franklin, Roger Sherman, James Madison, John Jay, John Dickinson, and Gouverneur Morris. Even Thomas Jefferson and John Adams, serving abroad as ambassadors, made their presence felt by writing to their followers.

Newspapers, the media of the day, featured a series of position papers and analyses of proposed articles written by Madison, Jay, and Alexander Hamilton under the pen name Publius. Collectively known as *The Federalist Papers*, these commentaries proved both erudite and influential.

The preamble (as drawn from the Declaration of Independence) set the tone by declaring that the people were establishing government for *their* purposes and that the government's source of existence was the *"consent of the People."*

The Constitution of the United States* was signed on September 17, 1787, and forwarded to the states for ratification. It contains only seven Articles:

Article I establishes a bicameral Congress, the House of Representatives and the Senate.

Article II vests executive power in the office of the President.

Article III establishes the Supreme Court.

Each article details the functions, limitations, and rules pertaining to that branch of government. Collectively, the first three articles set out the division of power between the legislative, executive and judicial branches, thus erecting barriers against the unchecked power of any governmental body.

*For your reference, the Constitution of the United States and its twenty-six amendments are reprinted in Appendices B and C, respectively.

Articles IV through VII cover general provisions and rules dealing with such concerns as the admission of new states, extradition rights, the addition of amendments to the Constitution, et al. They were attempting to establish a *limited* government, one that would referee rather than rule. (The referees in a modern football game *interpret* the rules of the game. They are not permitted to *change* the rules or to make new ones as they go along.)

Lord Acton believed that "The power to tax is the power to destroy." For that very reason there was furious debate over Article I, Section 8, of the Constitution. Known as the taxation clause, it strikes at a very delicate area, because much of the man-government relationship hinges on property rights. It reads (and please note the punctuation, because that semicolon may be the most significant in the history of the world):

> *The Congress shall have the power to lay and collect taxes, duties, imposts and excises, to pay the debts and provide for the common defense and general welfare of the united states; . . .*

That semicolon—*not a period*—is followed by a list of seventeen specific purposes for which the Congress is empowered to tax. The list that succeeds it was most deliberately compiled, and the founders intended to limit federal taxing powers to those purposes.

Since the early 1930s, there has been a tendency in our government to interpret the phrases *"promote the general welfare"* in the Preamble and *"general welfare"* in Article I, Section 8, as carte blanche authorization to tax for any purpose whatsoever. But that list makes it very clear that the founders would quarrel with such loose interpretation.

In Federalist Paper 41, James Madison replies to objections to the wording of that Article:

But what color can the objection have, when a specification of the objects alluded to by these general terms immediately follows, and is not even separated by a longer pause than a semi-colon? If the different parts of the same instrument ought to be so expounded, as to give meaning to every part which will bear it, shall one part of the same sentence be excluded altogether from a share in the meaning; and shall the more doubtful and indefinite terms be retained in their full extent, and the clear and precise expressions be denied any signification whatsoever? For what purpose could the enumeration of particular powers be inserted, if these and all others were meant to be included in the preceding general power? Nothing is more natural or common than first to use a general phrase, and then to explain and qualify it by a recital of particulars.

In Federalist Paper 45, he continues in the same vein:

The Powers delegated by the proposed Constitution to the Federal Government are few and defined. Those which are to remain to the state governments are numerous and indefinite. The former will be exercised on external objects, as war, peace, negotiations and foreign commerce; with which last the power of taxation will, for the most part, be connected. The powers reserved to the several states will extend to all the objects which, in the ordinary course of affairs, concern the lives, liberties, and properties of the people, and the internal order, improvement and prosperity of the state.[3]

So anxious were the framers to prevent such deviations as European "head taxes" that they added Article I, Section 9, sub-section 4, as further protection. It states: *"No Capitation, or other direct, Tax shall be laid"*—referring to income or head taxes.

Thanks to their precautions, the new nation's entrepreneurial economy exploded and in the next 188 years outdistanced and amazed the rest of the world.

As for the Preamble's phrase *"promote the general Welfare,"* the founders' principles and the entire tone of the Constitution support the conclusion that they meant to convey government's obligation to protect individuals from violence against their persons and property so that they might promote their own welfare without interference. They assuredly did not intend the clause as an open-ended authorization for Congress to redistribute the fruits of people's labor for any and all purposes.[4]

This brilliant document is the basis for a "free and ordered society." Nothing approached it at the time it was drafted, and nothing has approached it since. In order for us to understand, appreciate, and evaluate its provisions, we need to examine other aspects of man's relationship to government.

Notes

1. Frederic Bastiat, *The Law,* trans. Dean Russell (Irvington-on-Hudson, N.Y.: Foundation for Economic Education, 1981).
2. Gregory Wolfe, *A New Dawn of Liberty* (Century City, Ca.: Salvatori, 1992).
3. Clinton Rossiter, ed., *The Federalist Papers* (New York: New American Library, 1961).
4. William M. Meigs, *The Growth of the Constitution* (New York: J.E. Lippincott, 1900).

CHAPTER FOUR

The Roots of Freedom

The ideas set forth in the Declaration of Independence, the Constitution, and the Bill of Rights—expressed in fewer than ten thousand words—gave birth to a miracle of human freedom undreamt of even by the men who wrote them. The discussion and debate and contention and compromise that eventually produced the Constitution are evidence that a great many ideas were put forward in the process of drafting and adopting that document. How did the authors evaluate these ideas? How did they distinguish between the valid and the false? Between the workable and the unworkable? Among the suggestions put forward must have been bad ideas as well as good ones—and the effects of either can be profound.

Karl Marx, with Friedrich Engels, propounded a bad idea in *The Communist Manifesto*. In less than a century, that idea spread across almost a third of the earth's surface, and in its name almost a third of the world's population was enslaved.

Like our founding fathers, Marx drew his ideas from countless sources. His theories of class struggle had been promulgated by Gaetano Filangieri in 1780, and later by Claude Adrien Helvétius, Jean Paul Marat, François Babeuf, the Comte de Saint-Simon, Augusto Midnet, Augustin Thierry, and Benjamin Disraeli. Marx and Engels' convictions about the "exploitation of man" and the "deterioration of the working class under capitalism" came from the writings of Armand Bazaard, Prosper Enfantin, Pierre-Joseph Proudhon, and Antonio Genovesi. Bad ideas are as easily disseminated as good ones, and it is our good fortune that our founders had the wisdom to draw from superior sources.

The measurement of anything, including an idea, requires an agreed-upon standard. In the realm of ideas, the search for right principles—for standards—is an ongoing process. We often measure abstractions (e.g., freedom, responsibility) against historical precedents. Indeed, the great Roman legislator and orator Marcus Tullius Cicero declared:

> Not to know what has been transacted in former times is to be always a child. If no use is made of the labors of past ages, the world must remain always in the infancy of knowledge.

Like Janus, the Roman god with two faces, we look to the past with one pair of eyes and peer into the future with the other. What do we perceive as we view the past? Mankind has always struggled for survival. Through most of history, most of the human family has been ill-fed, ill-clothed, and ill-housed. Yet, in less than 160 years, in an area covering approximately 7 percent of the world's land, 6 percent of the world's population produced more than half of all the world's food and manufactured products. From log cabins to air-conditioned homes; from ox-carts to automobiles and airplanes, the miracle unfolded. Why and how did this happen?

Did America have greater natural resources than Europe or China or South America? No. More tools? No. Our early pioneers had little more than axes with which to clear the land. Let's take a closer look.

During most of man's history, he lived under what we used to call the pagan concept, the doctrine that man was helpless;

that he was wholly at the mercy of forces beyond his control. In short, he felt neither responsibility for his actions nor control of his future.

The American idea, however, was rooted in the Ten Commandments, received from God by Moses on Mount Sinai. Man was a free, self-controlling individual responsible for his own thoughts, words, and actions. And this code said that man received his right to property from God, not from other men or from the government. "Thou shalt not steal" from the Ten Commandments seems to prove that property was a God-given right.

Whether or not one believes in God, it is obvious that man was here first, before the government or state, and that his life or property could not possibly have been a gift of either. As the brilliant French political scientist Frederic Bastiat put it, "Life, liberty, property do not exist because man made laws. On the contrary, it was the fact that life, liberty, and property existed beforehand that caused men to make laws in the first place."

Defining Freedom

Unfortunately, the term "freedom" has been so misused that it now requires definition. What is the difference between freedom and license? Between "to covet" and "to aspire"? Do we have freedom *to?* Or freedom *from?*

Dr. Edmund Opitz, a distinguished scholar with the Foundation for Economic Education, says, "Freedom is a complicated subject. How, otherwise, could we account for the fact that man has had so little of it during the checkered history of this planet?"[1]

Just what *do* we mean by the term "individual freedom"?

History is the story of man-government relationships: strong governments, one-man rule, government ownership of the means of production, government control of the means of production, government-guaranteed security, ad infinitum. Many of these relationships have paid lip service to freedom. Hitler justified his aggression by invoking the German people's need for freedom; Stalin and Khrushchev constantly spoke of the freedom of the Soviet people, despite the brutal repressions they carried out; Mao Tse-tung, in *China's New Democracy* (1944) and in his many orations, referred frequently to the freedom of the Chinese people; and Fidel Castro took to the Sierra Maestra to fight for the Cuba's freedom.

The 1962 *Constitution of the Union of Soviet Socialist Republics* usually jolts readers unfamiliar with it, because it guarantees its citizens considerably more freedom than does our own Constitution:

- Article 125 guarantees freedom of speech, freedom of assembly (including mass meetings), and freedom to organize street protests and demonstrations.
- Article 124 guarantees freedom of religion.
- Article 118 guarantees employment and security in economic crises.
- Article 119 guarantees the right to rest and leisure, and provides access to sanatoria, rest homes, and clubs.
- Article 120 guarantees free medical care, access to health resorts, and maintenance in old age.
- Article 121 guarantees the right to an education.
- Article 122 guarantees equal rights for women and provides state aid for mothers of large families and for unwed mothers.[2]

By contrast, our own Constitution seems to short-change us. It guarantees none of those things in its initial form, and only a very few of them in its amendments. On closer investigation, however, we find that the Soviet Constitution, for all its guaranteed rights and freedoms, does not afford its citizens genuine human liberty. Instead, it clearly designates the state as the source of all rights and freedoms. In other words, freedom is a gift of the state. And what the state can give, the state can also take away.

The absence of any reference to spiritual values in the Soviet list is no accident. The political collective undermines its own power if it acknowledges the validity of spiritual faith. People who believe their rights derive from their Creator will reject the ascendancy of government above its proper position. On that basis, our founders restricted the powers of government, allowing it to exercise only such force as any individual is morally entitled to employ: An individual has the moral right to defend his own life, liberty, and property against fraud, violence, misrepresentation, and predation by others. Government has just such powers and no more. It was James Madison who specified that a government should exercise no more power over an individual than that individual should exercise over another person.

Human Rights and Government Functions

Let's explore the implications of Madison's dictum. I clearly have the right to defend my life and property if you attempt to take them. And vice versa. What's more, we have the right to cooperate in defending our lives and property against any other person or group of people. These are inherent human rights which have nothing to do with government. It is significant that these are *defensive* rights. I do *not* have the right to attack you; you do *not* have the right to attack me; and we do *not* have the right to join forces and attack anyone else.

Since we share these defensive rights in equal measure, we are free to entrust this defensive function to a third person or force (e.g., the government). By doing so, we relieve ourselves of the necessity of carrying guns, maintaining surveillance, or otherwise preparing to defend our own lives and property. It is, obviously, customary for people to give government the responsibility for protecting them from one another by creating police forces and from outside aggression by training and arming a military. Individuals may or may not agree with the cost or specific structure of this defense at times, but there is no moral argument against a legitimate government's exercise of defensive functions.

Likewise, a court system is empowered to establish justice

and arbitrate our disagreements, and this too is a logical and moral function of government. Again, individuals may disagree with the judgment of the courts, but their existence is morally both right and necessary.

I do not have the right to force you to join a club, and you do not have the right to force me to join a church. Indeed, I have no right to force you to do anything, because the only force I can morally employ is *defensive*.

This brings us to a crucial issue: If I cannot force you to do a thing, how can I empower a government, for example, to force you to join a union in order to keep your job?

I have no right to take a percentage of what you earn each month—not even if I promise to return it to you when you are sixty-five. So how can I possibly pass on to government the power to enact and enforce mandatory Social Security? (NB: This has nothing to do with whether membership in Social Security is a good or bad idea. It is simply a question of whether such membership can be mandatory.)

Ezra Taft Benson, Eisenhower's secretary of agriculture and past president of the Council of Twelve of the Church of Jesus Christ of Latter Day Saints, once wrote:

> A government is nothing more or less than a group of citizens who have been hired by the rest of us to perform certain responsibilities which have been authorized. The government itself has no innate power or privilege to do anything. Its only source of authority and power is from the people who created it.
>
> Keep in mind that the people who have created the government can give that government only such powers as they themselves have. They cannot give that which they do not possess.
>
> In a primitive state, there is no doubt that each man would be justified in using force, if necessary, to defend himself against physical harm, against theft of the fruits of his labor, and against enslavement by another.

Indeed, the early pioneers found that a great deal of their time and energy was being spent defending themselves, their property, and their liberty. For a man to prosper, he cannot afford to spend his time constantly guarding his family, his fields, and his property against attack and theft. When he joins together with his neighbors and hires a sheriff, government is born. The individual citizens delegate to the sheriff their unquestionable right to protect themselves. The sheriff now does for them only that which they had the right to do for themselves—nothing more.

But, suppose pioneer "A" wants another horse for his wagon. He doesn't have the money to buy one, but, since pioneer "B" has an extra horse, he decides he is entitled to share his neighbor's good fortune. Is he entitled to take his neighbor's horse? Obviously not! If his neighbor wishes to give it or lend it, that is another question. But so long as pioneer "B" wishes to keep his property, pioneer "A" has no claim to it.

If "A" has no proper power to take "B's" property, can he delegate any such power to the sheriff? No! Even if everyone in the community desires that "B" give his extra horse to "A," they have no right, individually or collectively, to force him to do it.

They cannot delegate a power they themselves do not have. The creation cannot exceed the creator.[3]

Any individual is free to act creatively and productively so long as he does not improperly infringe on the equal rights of others. This, then, is the difference between freedom and license: Freedom cannot exist without responsibility. License is the [alleged] unrestrained right to do as one pleases. When that infringes on the rights of another, it becomes tyranny.

It follows from these principles that government is also excluded from any action beyond securing the rights with which we have been endowed by our Creator. It has no right to tamper with or manage any creative activity.

We have examined in the light of historical experience the principles against which the work of our founders must be measured. Now we will examine the natural forces at work in the man-government relationship.

Human Nature and the Nature of Government

My business, involving the design and engineering of products, made it necessary to consider the elements being combined to achieve the desired result. In that activity, the characteristics of the materials selected are critical. There are no skyscrapers built of butter and no bridges constructed of rubber. In the design and engineering of a formula involving man-government relationship, then, the first order of business is to consider the nature of each.

First, human beings are not perfect. They are flawed in both character and judgment. Their knowledge is limited, and their perceptions are often skewed. Sometimes, then, they fail to accurately assess their own limitations—to realize that they are not perfect.

Second, men are not equal except in the eyes of God and, therefore, in the eyes of the law. In his *Politics*, Aristotle asserted, "The only stable state is one in which all men are equal before the law." This equality applies to rights, privileges, and treatment. And it is naturally ordained.

Nature treats her creatures equally under the laws of the universe, but they are not equal in any other sense. As Emerson observed, "Nature never rhymes her children nor makes two alike." Lions are stronger than chipmunks; eland run faster than buffalo; and dolphins are smarter than starfish. Human beings are not equal in size, shape, talent, aspirations, or ability, and they strive to achieve even greater inequality. Writers and speakers often refer to the "common man," but who places himself in that category? What's more, people want a very uncommon doctor when they are ill, a very uncommon lawyer when they are in legal difficulty, and a very uncommon general when they are attacked or invaded.

So—human beings are not perfect, and they differ widely, one from another. That is the nature of man.

As to the nature of government: In most societies, government has functioned by force. Citizens of Assyria, Persia, Egypt, Greece, Rome, medieval Italy, Bourbon France, Elizabethan England, the Indian Raj, Nazi Germany and Soviet Russia, all submitted to state power. In these civilizations, state power was pervasive, overwhelming individual liberty. Societies—including those mentioned above—initially created or permitted the growth of government power to meet defensive needs. That power eventually expanded beyond its policing or peacekeeping functions and became oppressive.

Government, after all, is made up of imperfect human beings and involves the allocation of power. Thus, the study of government is, at one level, the study of power and of its effect on both the controllers and the controlled. History proves that power is a heady wine and can have tragic results for humanity. Lord Acton's dictum, "Power tends to corrupt, and absolute power corrupts absolutely," appears to be as immutable as the law of gravity.

Power may be won, usurped, seized, or delegated, but how it is obtained is less important than how it is used. Excessive power is bad, whether in business, labor, or government. Of the three, however, government has the worst record, because it is backed by the strongest force.

On its own, neither the imperfect nature of man nor the power of government is particularly dangerous. But the combination can be deadly, because man's imperfections are magnified by the acquisition of power.

Intentions have little or nothing to do with the destructive nature and consequences of power. History is full of benevolent dictators. Su Tungpo, an eleventh century Chinese poet-historian, wrote that "Nothing is so dangerous to a Nation's destiny as an opinionated, but misguided idealist."[4]

Still, if human beings are so imperfect, shouldn't someone

protect them from others and from themselves? Who? A government? But that government itself will be made up of imperfect men. Were Lyndon Johnson, Theodore Roosevelt, Abraham Lincoln, John F. Kennedy, Herbert Hoover, and Franklin D. Roosevelt perfect? Does an imperfect man shed his weaknesses when he assumes public office? Obviously not.

After all, if "the common man" (or woman) blunders, the effect is visited on a family, a neighborhood, perhaps even a business and its customers and suppliers. If the head of a government errs, his actions or decisions can affect an entire nation and—in the case of a leading nation—the entire world. Nevertheless, we have to entrust our government to imperfect human beings. It is, therefore, essential that we keep close watch over our endowed rights. The danger to them lies less in open and outright attempts to enslave us than in subtle, slow dilution of those rights. We must, in effect, not become so watchful for muggers that we are oblivious to pickpockets. Thomas Jefferson put it best: "When it comes to questions of power, let no more be heard of the goodness of man, but bind him down with the chains of the Constitution."

The Right to Hold Property
Former Supreme Court Justice George Sutherland issued this warning:

> The individual has three rights, equally sacred from arbitrary interference: the right to his life, the right to his property, the right to his liberty. These three rights are so bound together as to be essentially one right. To give a man his life, but to deny him his liberty, is to take from him all that makes his life worth living. To give him his liberty, but to take from him his property which is the fruit and badge of his liberty, is to still leave him a slave.[5]

Not everything in our lives is a right. Does anyone have the right to an education? The right to adequate food, clothing, and housing? The right to a car, a TV set, an automatic washer and dryer? The right to a job? Or are these things actually economic goals?

In fact, our only endowed rights are the rights to life, to the freedom to sustain life, and to acquire and/or hold private property. In some academic discussions, rights are divided into two categories—human rights and property rights. But the right to hold property—property not obtained by force, coercion, or fraud—*is* a human right. Which brings us to the sources and nature of property. We are accustomed to hearing that this or that project will be accomplished and paid for by the government, but how can that be? Governments do not create wealth. Wealth is created by investors and workers: the stockholders, the chairman of the board, the janitor, the lathe operator, the salesman, the engineer, etc. All a government can do is distribute or redistribute what people create.

True, government can direct economic activity by hiring or extending contracts to people in the private sector, but it is the private sector that creates the wealth. Taxpayers simply exchange their goods and services for the wealth created. The government is a middleman who adds considerable additional cost to the transaction but creates no wealth.

What sources are available to individuals in search of material things— e.g., food, clothing, personal computers, golf clubs, yachts?

1. They can work, earn, create, or inherit property—or exchange one property for another. None requires fraud or coercion.
2. They can steal from others who have acquired the property honestly. This requires fraud or coercion.

In short, they can create or plunder.[6] Plundering, unfortunately, has been the option of choice for many people in every society, and it is one of the logical and moral functions of government to protect this basic human right by preventing such plundering.

If I redistribute property or income in my neighborhood by force, I am committing an immoral act and a crime. If I hire a professional gangster to do the job for me, I am still breaking the natural and the civil law. What if I hire the government to do it for me? Am I any less guilty? Does "Thou shalt not steal" apply to some people and not to others? To man but not to government?

If laws are passed to sanction such forced redistribution, don't they simply legalize plundering? If such laws are approved by a majority, does this make them right?

The philosophical question is, "Can you create a good society made up of imperfect people?" Some would say that that amounts to asking a chef, "Can you create a good omelet out of bad eggs?" But there is a major difference that appears as soon as one goes on to ask, "Can you improve the quality of the eggs? Can you improve the quality of the people?" The eggs, once in the omelet, are there for better or for worse. But people can and do change. Indeed, the same person will behave differently in different circumstances.

Individual Responsibility

So the question becomes "Under what conditions does man behave at the highest level of morality and responsibility?" Society is made up of individuals, and the attitudes and actions of society simply reflect those of the individuals who compose it. Mob psychology demonstrates that most people behave better when they function as individuals subject to the dictates of their consciences than when they act as members of a group. People behave best when they must face the consequences of their actions.

We tend to assume our highest level of behavior when, as individuals, we find ourselves in the position of having to face directly the consequences of our actions. Ergo, the environment in which people display the highest level of behavior is one that encourages—even demands—individual responsibility. By contrast, a person can escape the feeling of responsibility when, as a member of a group, he can consciously or subconsciously "pass the buck."

By way of example: I am not about to sing a solo in church and take personal responsibility for the reaction of the rest of the congregation. However, when the whole congregation sings out with Sunday morning enthusiasm, I join in without hesitation because the responsibility is shared or diluted (and maybe no one will be certain who is off-key).

On a more serious level, how many people would take another's life, other than in self-defense? But how many would stand on the fringes of a lynch mob, blaming the action on the other people or rationalizing their own participation as accepting the will of the majority?

Now suppose you are a farmer. You have just received a letter from the Department of Agriculture advising that you are entitled to a payment of $5,000 for participating in the soil-bank program (i.e., for *not raising* certain crops). Suppose the letter indicates that you will no longer receive your usual check. Instead, the government agency will furnish you with a list of taxpayers from whom you can collect your subsidy. (You may ask your local police department to support your claims, if necessary.) You are authorized to collect $850 from Bill Brown of 436 Maple Street, $990 from Henry Smith of 1429 Henderson Avenue, $1,100 from John Ford of 123 Main Street, $685 from Helen Stewart of 1215 Fourth Street, etc.—for a total collection of $5,000.

Would you accept this arrangement? Probably not. Because you would be forced to look those people in the eye and ask them to pay you for something you *didn't do*. They would be asked to hand you money, and you would give them nothing in return. And they would know who you were.

What happens when a bureaucracy removes the necessity of facing the reality of our actions? When it does the collecting for us—by force? This "money laundering" cleanses the transaction of its unsavory nature. Even people who initially question the action end up rationalizing: "It isn't my fault! It's the government . . . or other farmers . . . or Peter Rabbit . . . or sun spots." And they take the money.

That's just one illustration of a fundamental fact: The only way to raise the quality of people's morals is by establishing an environment that encourages individual responsibility. No society, no group, no nation possesses integrity, wisdom, justice, morality, or a sense of responsibility. These traits reside only in individuals, and only individuals can acquire them.

Why the Majority *Doesn't* Rule

Individuals are also the functioning pieces of a majority. Majority rule is often misunderstood to be the basis of democracy, and we are told that we live in a democracy. Our children study from textbooks entitled *Problem Solving in Our American Democracy*. We were taught that World War I was fought "To make the world safe for democracy." By now, the term has acquired an almost sacred connotation.

This reverence and this reference persist in spite of the fact that the word does not appear in any of our basic documents—the Declaration of Independence, the Constitution, or the Bill of Rights. Indeed, our founders expressed vigorous fear of and disdain for political democracy, impressed as they were by the downfall of ancient Greece and of the Roman Empire.

Why this current infatuation with democracy?

For one thing, our society has a certain respect for majority opinion, as though the will of the majority could distinguish right from wrong. Recent U.S. political history finds both parties and candidates genuflecting to the opinions gleaned from polling. It sometimes seems that if a major TV network reported that 51 percent of the American people wanted all Catholics taller than 5'8" beheaded, many politicians would consider the proposition. In *Emerson in Suburbia*, Samuel Withers writes:

> Emerson's voice cried out, "Nothing is at last sacred but the integrity of your own mind," and Suburbia's voices

would chorus in reply, "Nothing is at last sacred but the collective will of the people."

It is important to question majority rule on several counts. Christ and Socrates were put to death in deference to majorities. Our own founders would probably have been hanged with the approval of the majority if they had failed to establish our independence.

Those founders were as fearful of the tyranny of the majority as of the tyranny of a king. And fear of tyranny was paramount in the minds of the men who established and secured our liberties. They carefully constructed mechanisms to restrict any encroachment by a majority upon the rights of a minority (e.g., the president's veto power over a bill passed by a majority of legislators).

Almost two hundred years ago, Professor Alexander Fraser Tytler suggested that a democracy cannot exist as a permanent form of government. It can exist, he believed, only until the voters discover that they can vote themselves largess out of the public treasury. From that moment on, the majority will always vote for the candidate promising the most benefits from the public treasury with the result that the democracy always collapses from a loose fiscal policy—and is followed by a dictatorship. A bleak outlook, but an important warning against majority rule.

Decisions founded on individual conscience, integrity, reason, and principle are of a higher order than those arrived at by sheer numbers. A majority cannot possess these qualities. They belong only to individuals.

We do not decide medical questions, engineering design, or mathematical equations by majority vote. We examine principles, facts, and laws of nature. Can we then leave moral questions to the caprice of the majority? Leonard Read stated it well in his *Conscience of the Majority:*

> Majority support does not remove coercion or force; it does tend to remove conscience. Whatever goodness may

be manifested in individual action tends to be lost in mass action.[7]

What's more, majority rule is still *rule*. Under the principles adopted by our founding fathers, the entire concept of "rule" was rejected in the interest of maintaining individual liberty. As applied to the election of public officials, acceding to the will of the majority probably has more in its favor than against it, but under our system of government, election to office does not constitute a "right to rule."

Understanding the function of the majority depends on an understanding of the source of government power in a free society—the people. No doubt some of the confusion surrounding the term *democracy* arises from our wholesome acceptance of the concept in its social applications. The elimination of titles denoting royalty and the destruction of the caste system are healthy means of endorsing human equality under the law.

Summary

This discussion has provided questions we can apply to evaluate the ideas the founders incorporated into our Declaration of Independence, Constitution, and Bill of Rights. Happily, the same questions can be applied to any piece of legislation currently before the Congress:

1. Does this idea promote or impede individual freedom and creativity?
2. Is this idea consistent with the recognition that all men are imperfect?
3. Does this idea increase or decrease the power of some men over others?
4. Does this idea acknowledge the inability of government to create wealth?
5. Does this idea authorize taking property from one person and giving it to others?
6. Does this idea encourage or discourage individual responsibility?

7. Does this idea allow government to do something which, if done by an individual, would constitute a crime?

I believe that we can apply these questions to constitutional provisions to decide whether they are based on valid principles. I do not suggest that these documents are perfect. Any formula for a man-government relationship must not only be valid and workable at the time it is devised, but must remain so for succeeding generations.

The Preamble, for instance, definitely sets the right tone:

WE THE PEOPLE of the United States, in Order to form a more perfect Union, establish Justice, insure domestic Tranquillity, provide for the common defence, promote the general Welfare, and secure the Blessings of Liberty to ourselves and our Posterity, do ordain and establish this Constitution for the United States of America.

Our court system was devised to *"establish justice."* The courts act as an objective third party to arbitrate disputes, thus grounding the government in law rather than in any person (recognizing the imperfection of human beings).

Police forces and the military exist to *"insure domestic Tranquillity, [and] provide for the common defence."* They protect our endowed rights from one another and from outside interference, leaving us free to exercise our talents. But they are under control of civilian authorities (i.e., mayors and city councils in the case of the police; Congress and the president in the case of the military) who are answerable to the electorate.

We noted earlier that government should encourage individual responsibility. By so doing, it *"promote[s] the general Welfare."* (This particular provision, touched on in Chapter 3, has been very broadly interpreted, and we will consider it more fully in a later chapter.)

The Roots of Freedom

The Constitution is, more than anything else, a set of limitations on the power of the federal government. The Bill of Rights provides additional support for this contention in the ninth and tenth amendments:

Amendment IX
The enumeration in the Constitution, of certain rights, shall not be construed to deny or disparage others retained by the people.

Amendment X
The powers not delegated to the United States by the Constitution, nor prohibited by it to the States, are reserved to the States respectively, or to the people.

The first ten amendments (the Bill of Rights) as ratified on December 15, 1791, were added to advance the principles underlying individual liberty.

Notes
1. Edmund A. Opitz, *Defining Freedom*, (Irvington-on-Hudson, N.Y.: Foundation for Economic Education, 1963).
2. *Constitution of the Union of Soviet Socialist Republics* (Moscow: Foreign Language Publishing House, 1962).
3. Ezra Taft Benson, *The Proper Role of Government* (Irvington-on-Hudson, N.Y.: Foundation for Economic Education, 1956).
4. Yu-T'ang Lin, *The Gay Genius*, (Westport, Conn.: Greenwood, 1948).
5. Justice George Sutherland, *Constitutional Power and World Affairs* (New York: Columbia University Press, 1919).
6. Bastiat, *The Law*.
7. Leonard E. Read, *Conscience of the Majority* (Irvington-on-Hudson, N.Y.: Foundation for Economic Education, 1963)

CHAPTER FIVE

The Test of Time

Our Constitution, then, is based on sound principles, and, though written by imperfect human beings and therefore imperfect, it surpasses by a wide margin any other attempt to codify the principles of human liberty.

How have those principles fared over the two-centuries-plus since the Constitution was adopted? Have government growth and government power been properly controlled? To find an answer to those questions, consider how Thomas Jefferson, in his first inaugural address, defined the aims of his administration:

> A wise and frugal government which shall restrain men from injuring one another, shall leave them otherwise free to regulate their own pursuits of industry and improve them and shall not take from the mouth of labor the bread it has earned. This is the sum of good government.

Jefferson's view of the role of government respects the tradition of individual liberty. What has happened to that role in the intervening years?

1. Have ensuing amendments altered to any degree the basic intent of the document?

2. Have there been changes in the interpretation and application of the fundamental provisions that limit the power of centralized government?
3. Have such changes had a beneficial or deleterious effect on our culture and on the behavior of our people?

Our primary analysis in this area will focus on those amendments ratified after the adoption of the Bill of Rights, but we begin with a look at the First Amendment.

The First Amendment

Congress shall make no law respecting an establishment of religion, or prohibiting the free exercise thereof; . . . .

What has come to be called the "establishment clause" in the Bill of Rights is a good example of the freedom-from/freedom-to distinction discussed in Chapter 4. Did the founders intend us to have the freedom *to* worship as we wish? Or did they mean to give us freedom *from* worship? We don't have to look far for an answer. John Adams wrote, *"Our Constitution was made only for a moral and religious people. It is wholly inadequate to the government of any other."* And Thomas Jefferson put it even more definitively:

We have staked the whole future of American civilization not upon the power of government. We have staked the future of all of our political constitutions upon the capacity of each and all of us to govern ourselves according to the Ten Commandments.

Neither comment should surprise us. The principles of American government and society were laid down in the Judaeo-Christian tradition. Indeed, the doctrines of human freedom and limited government were introduced by such Christian theologians such as St. Augustine of Hippo and St. Thomas Aquinas.

When a young French gentleman, Alexis de Tocqueville,

came to America in the 1840s, it was clear that the American people shared Adams' and Jefferson's convictions. Tocqueville wrote:

> I sought for the greatness and genius of America in fertile fields and boundless forests; it was not there. I sought for it in her free schools and her institutions of learning; it was not there. I sought for it in her matchless Constitution and democratic congress; it was not there. Not until I went to the churches of America and found them aflame with righteousness did I understand the greatness and genius of America. America is great because America is good. When America ceases to be good, America will cease to be great.[1]

Please note carefully both the wording and the intent of Amendment I: The phrase "separation of church and state" does not appear. The founders' sole intent was to prevent any one religious denomination from becoming *the* government-sponsored religion. And in cases in heard in 1796, 1811, 1844, 1892, and 1931, the Supreme Court affirmed that intention.

Then the Court decided to legislate. Look at the rulings listed below, and at the dates they were issued:

1947 Mandated separation of church and state.

1962 Banned prayer in school

1963 Banned reading of the Bible in school

1967 Banned the audible saying of grace by students in school lunchrooms

1967 Banned the reading in public schools of a nursery rhyme. The verse in question did not even mention God, but the court said, "Although the word God is not contained in the nursery rhyme, if someone were to hear it, it might cause them to think of God and it is therefore unconstitutional."[2]

1980 With the case of *Stone v. Graham*, the posting of the Ten Commandments in our public school systems became illegal. The Supreme Court said, "If the posted copies of the Ten Commandments are to have any effect at all it will be to induce the school children to read them, and if they read them they may meditate upon them and perhaps venerate and obey them. This is not a permissible objective."

The First Amendment, properly understood, definitively supports the intent of the Constitution. On that basis alone, John Adams' statement and Tocqueville's prediction should give us pause when we observe how much of our population has forsaken the practice of religion and realize how thoroughly religion has been removed from most aspects of our lives.

Just one example: One of the primary sources employed by the founding fathers was Sir William Blackstone's *Commentaries on the Law*. For some 160 years this was a primary text in every law school in the United States. Every case or law cited in it was cross-referenced with Bible verses related to that law. But though *Blackstone's Commentaries* remains a legal classic, it is no longer a staple of the law school curriculum.

During the 176 years between 1791 and 1967 only sixteen amendments were added to the original ten that constituted the Bill of Rights: Amendment XIII abolished slavery; Amendment XV guaranteed the right to vote regardless of race, color, or previous condition of servitude; and Amendment XIX guaranteed the right to vote regardless of sex.

Each of these is fully in accord with the intent of the founders, because each is based on a fundamental understanding of human liberty as an inherent right.

The Sixteenth Amendment

Only Amendment XVI, generally referred to as the Income Tax Amendment, drastically altered the original intent of the Constitution with respect to citizens' rights:

The Congress shall have power to lay and collect taxes on incomes, from whatever source derived, without apportionment among the several States, and without regard to any census or enumeration.

The American people recognized the need for taxes to fund legitimate government activities, but the idea of government taking the fruits of one's labor—and of taking more from the more productive—was new. During the Civil War, an emergency-based income tax was levied but it was promptly abolished when the war ended.

The Sixteenth Amendment debate in Congress and throughout the nation was furious. Previous Supreme Court rulings had declared income taxes unconstitutional, and this amendment did not even limit the amount of the tax. The amendment's proponents in Congress promised that the top tax rate would never exceed 10 percent, and it was passed into law. If you read the debate, however, you will see that the amendment passed only because of the consensus that such a tax *would never exceed 2.5 percent* on any but the very rich.

The provisions of the original tax make interesting reading. The personal exemption was $3,000 ($34,400 in today's dollars) for a single person and $4,000 ($45,900 today) for a married couple. Higher incomes were taxed at 1 percent, and people with incomes over $500,000 (over $5.5 million today) paid an astonishing 6 percent tax.[3]

The intent of the tax was to penalize the so-called robber barons. In theory only the rich would pay, and in fact fewer than one person in every seven even filed. Under such conditions, perhaps it is understandable that no one foresaw how the concept would eventually threaten the middle-class wage earner. In addition to the Pandora's box opened by the adoption of the Sixteenth Amendment, it clearly violated the intent of Article I, Section 8, and Article I, Section 9, sub-section 4.*

*See Appendix B.

The original debate over the "taxation clause" of the Constitution itself was resolved by restricting the power to *"lay and collect Taxes, Duties, Imposts and Excises"* to very specific areas. Section 9, sub-section 4, was added to protect the fruits of one's labor from any form of income tax.

Obviously the government is not functioning within the parameters set by the Constitution. The basic intent of the Constitution *was altered* to a major degree by the Sixteenth Amendment; serious changes in interpretation *have* weakened the application of its fundamental principles; and the consequences have had a *negative* effect on our culture and on the behavior of our people.

The Constitution has been contorted by politicians poorly schooled in the history, principles, and traditions of this nation, and by an uneducated and apathetic public that takes the blessings of liberty for granted.

To quote Professor Walter Williams,

> The White House and the Supreme Court appear to have abiding contempt for the Constitution; ... Today the 9th and 10th Amendments have been completely trashed and the 2nd and 5th Amendments are under attack. We Americans are left with a Constitutional carcass.[4]

Notes

1. Alexis de Tocqueville, *Democracy in America* (New York: Oxford University Press, 1952).
2. David Moore, *America, You're Too Young to Die* (Summerland, Ga.: Harbour House [West], 1994).
3. Walter Williams, *Conservative Chronicle* (Hampton, 1995).
4. Ibid.

CHAPTER SIX

Why Government Grows

In 1936, 160 years after the Declaration of Independence was signed, the profligate spending of Roosevelt's New Deal introduced deficit financing. Nevertheless, even under the stresses created by the Great Depression, F.D.R. spent less than 8 percent of the gross domestic product. World War II cost billions. The Marshall Plan for the postwar rebuilding of Europe required an enormous financial outlay, as did the GI Bill of Rights, which sent thousands of veterans through college. Before the country could recover its economic equilibrium, the Korean War was under way. Yet even under those extraordinary circumstances, President Truman produced a budget surplus. Still, during this period the seeds of government expansion were sown and the erosion of some of our constitutional principles began. From academia and from the inner sanctums of government itself came challenges to the spirit and the letter of our founding documents.

But in 1960, after two terms of the Eisenhower administration, the nation appeared on the surface to be healthy: Taxes were relatively reasonable, American workers commanded the highest hourly wages in the world, and the national debt was lower in real dollars than it had been at the end of World War II.

Then, between 1962 and 1995, our government expenditures grew 423 times as much as our population. The number of government employees at all levels (federal, state, and local) grew at 6 times the rate of employees in the private sector. Federal, state, and local taxes multiplied 15 times in real dollars.

Before we examine the gory details that explain why all this happened to our government, we must ask the more general question, "Why do governments grow?"

Both history and logic tell us that any loss of economic freedom leads to a corresponding loss of personal freedom and to the depreciation of personal responsibility and morality. Whoever controls one's economic well-being will intervene to the same degree in one's personal life. Remember, the constitution of the former Soviet Union guaranteed every personal freedom imaginable, and yet Soviet citizens enjoyed very little personal liberty. Economic freedom didn't exist in the U.S.S.R., and , in the final analysis, property rights *are* human rights.

In 1913 a U.S. citizen was approximately 99 percent free in the sense that he could do as he wished with roughly 99 percent of his income. (Federal taxes totaled about 1 percent, except on the seven American millionaires who reported that year. They paid 7 percent.) Today that same citizen is less than 50 percent free to determine the disposition of his income.

Governments Control People

Freedom of religion is a hallowed American right, surely one that government should respect. Yet Amish citizens of Ohio had their livestock and other property confiscated by federal officials. Why? Because their religion does not permit them to contribute to, or receive money from, such programs as Social Security. That Amish community moved to Canada in search of religious liberty.

Since governments do not produce wealth, our government doesn't grow wheat. It does, however, tell U.S. farmers which of them may grow wheat, and how much. So, although the farmland belongs to the farmer (or to the landholder from whom he rents), the government controls how it is used.

Similarly, some sixteen million American workers *must* belong to labor unions whether they wish to or not, and their union dues are deducted from their paychecks before they receive them, just as if they were taxes. Government allows closed-shop laws to control the freedom of employers to hire whatever workers they choose.

At present, many of our personal freedoms remain relatively secure, but the examples above illustrate that our economic freedoms are under constant attack. In controlled economies, freedoms are always at risk. Conversely, where the economy is most free, freedom of the press, of speech, and of religion flourish.

Freedom Isn't Free

Surely, all of us favor individual liberty and wish to retain it, so why do we allow these encroachments?

Thomas à Kempis, the fifteenth-century author of the *Imitation of Christ* understood the problem: "All men favor individual freedom, but few men favor the things that make for individual freedom."

Individual responsibility is not an easy load to carry. Indeed, Dean Russell wrote:

> No one person is responsible for sapping the spirit of individualism. No one political party is to blame. The people are as responsible as the elected and appointed leaders. It is we the people who seem to have forgotten that freedom and responsibility are inseparable. It is we the people who are discarding the concept of government that brought forth the Declaration of Independence, the Constitution, and the Bill of Rights.
>
> In short, few of us seem to want to keep government out of our personal affairs and responsibilities. Many of us

seem to favor various types of government-guaranteed and compulsory "security." We boast that we are responsible persons, but we vote for candidates who promise us special privileges, government pensions, government subsidies, and government electricity.

Such schemes are directly contrary to the spirit of the Bill of Rights. Our heritage is being lost more through weakness than through deliberate design ... many of us are drifting back to that old concept of government that our forefathers feared and rejected. Many of us are no longer willing to accept individual responsibility for our own welfare. Yet personal freedom cannot exist without individual responsibility.[1]

What's more, we face the problem of sloppy semantics. Would most Americans accept the introduction of a program labeled *communism?* Or *socialism?* Or *regimentation?* But what if the program is called *welfare?* Or *security?* Or *social progress?* Then watch those voters grab the bait hook, line, and sinker.

In the early 1960s, Norman Thomas debated William F. Buckley, Jr. In part of his remarks, Thomas stated,

> I have run for President six times on the Socialist ticket and never managed to garner more than 7 percent of the popular vote. I'm happy to say, however, that almost every plank in my platform has been nailed firmly in place under legislation entitled "welfare" and "security" except medical care for the aged, and I fully expect that we'll have that very shortly.[2]

You must admire Thomas for his forthright honesty. His point is crystal clear.

The Absence of Attrition

Absence of attrition is another reason for government growth. In the free market, a product succeeds or fails depending on customer response. If the product doesn't sell, the business reacts accordingly. When automobiles became generally affordable, buggy-whip factories either went out of business or retooled to produce some more salable item.

If government were subject to the same forces, a department with a failed program would have to eliminate it. In fact, however, if a government program is ineffective, the government is likely to enlarge it (apparently in the belief that money added to manpower equals efficiency and effectiveness). Attrition is virtually unheard of.

One classic example is the Department of Agriculture's crop subsidy program. The number of farms in the United States has dropped by one third during the last half century, but the number of bureaucrats dealing with this farm program has tripled (at an annual cost to the taxpayers of $56 billion a year, not including the cost of the food stamp and Forest Service personnel who are now part of the department). If business operated the same way, there would be a buggy-whip shop in every strip mall.

By the way, it's also interesting that the crop-subsidy program applied to about 25 percent of farm products. The other—non-subsidized—75 percent have done very nicely without government intervention, and the subsidized crops have been in perpetual difficulty.

The ostensible purpose of crop subsidies was to help preserve small family farms. Instead, the big corporate farms have multiplied and flourished while the percentage of small, family farms has declined.[3] Which means that we have a product (crop subsidies) for which there is less demand (fewer farms), a product which does not work (non-subsidized crops fare better in the marketplace) and has not met its long-term goals (preserving family farms)—and therefore our business (the Department of Agriculture) is growing. The mind reels.

In a paper entitled "Why Government Grows," Professor Allan H. Meltzer of Carnegie-Mellon University suggests a very logical theory. Given a society with a sizable middle class and political representatives elected by popular vote, government will grow faster than the private sector whenever the costs of government can be diffused and the benefits concentrated. This condition creates incentives for expanding—and disincentives for reducing—the size of government. Special interests are strongly motivated to support a certain program because they profit greatly from it, and the general public (if it is even aware of the program) judges its cost to be relatively minor and therefore doesn't resist the program. When, on the other hand, taxes (costs) are concentrated and benefits diffused, a coalition in favor of tax reduction can be organized to eliminate the program.[4]

Meltzer goes on to explain that a competitive political process sustains efficient coalitions and eliminates inefficient coalitions. Those who favor tax reduction and smaller government can be diverted and/or converted if a program's sponsors can include benefits that reward its opponents—e.g., specific tax reductions, subsidies, regulation of competition, tariffs, licensing, pension plans, and schooling.

A free market allows entrepreneurs to buy inefficient businesses, improve their productivity, and reap the profit. The political process, on the other hand, offers little incentive to eliminate inefficiency, reduce the size of agencies and departments, and cut taxes. The benefits accruing to such reforms are so diffuse that no person or group is sufficiently motivated to demand them.

Consequently, there is a vast redistribution of wealth from the control of individual taxpayers to that of government employees. The percentage of the labor force employed by government has increased at about the same rate as the percentage of personal income paid in taxes. Both have more than doubled and redoubled in this century.

What Teachers Are Taught

Our system of public education has left two generations of Americans with a minimal awareness of the principles fundamental to a free and ordered society. The philosophy of a nation ought to be reflected in its educational system. However, any educational system will inevitably reflect the philosophy and attitudes of its teachers. And certainly the teachers of teachers will pass on *their* philosophy and attitudes. Especially if the schools of education become the "gatekeepers" to the teaching profession because state licensing requires all teachers to be trained at schools of education; and if teachers then are forced into powerful national unions as well. Then the "teachers of teachers" have the potential to become something they never have been in American history: promoters of a philosophy that may indeed not reflect the national culture. This, in a nutshell, is what happened to American education.

For example, consider five prominent "teachers of teachers": George S. Counts, Ph.D., Columbia University; John Dewey, Ph.D., the University of Chicago; William Kilpatrick, Ph.D., Columbia University; James Mendenhall, Ph.D., Columbia University; and Harold Rugg, Ph.D., Columbia University. Four of these gentlemen were officers of the Intercollegiate Society of Socialists, and four were graduates of Columbia University's Teacher's College. They were the architects of the wave of progressive education that swept the nation in the 1930s. Collectively, they wrote almost two hundred books and teachers' guides on education and social sciences. An estimated thirty million students have used their material.Their writings share a basic point of view:

1. In the new social order, educators must teach *what* to think, not *how* to think.
2. The American free enterprise system must be regarded as a failure.
3. We must eliminate the possibility of failure and strive for equalization and conformity.
4. Standards of excellence have no place in the new social order.

In Harold Rugg's best-known book, *The Great Technology* (1933), he states, "Our task is nothing short of questioning the whole philosophy of living, and philosophy of private capitalism and laissez faire." Elsewhere in the same book he says,

> We must uproot the deep-rooted loyalties of the American people to an entire culture lacking in integrity. It is clear, therefore, that if educational agencies are to be utilized in the production of a new social order, an indispensable first step is that of developing a totally new outlook upon life and education among the rank and file of teachers.

He refers to the story of the founding fathers and to U. S. history in these words:

> Nothing about this story of degradation is clearer than that, in any of those decades, a fairly decent standard of living could have been had by the peoples of the expanding west. That it was not, and is not today, can be traced primarily to the theory and practice of government set up by our fathers.

Finally, in a pamphlet entitled "Building a Science of Society for the Schools," Rugg made a chilling proposal:

> A new public mind is to be created. How? Only by creating tens of millions of individual minds and welding them into a new social mind. That is the task of the building of a science of society for the schools.

The regrettably prolific Rugg eventually produced fourteen textbooks, eight for elementary grades and six for junior high schools. It is disturbing to reflect on the effect they must have had on young minds.

Rugg and Mendenhall collaborated on a number of teachers' guides comprising what was called the Rugg-Mendenhall System. Under their regime there was no room for disagreement or debate in the classroom. The teacher was given the "correct" answers to the text questions and was told how to interpret historical facts and other material in the textbooks. For instance:

> **Q:** Is the United States a land of opportunity for all our people? Why?
>
> **A:** The United States is not a land of opportunity for all our people; for one fifth of the people do not earn any money at all. There are great differences in the standards of living of different classes of people. The majority do not have any real security.
>
> Treat the War for Independence essentially as an economic struggle between the ruling classes of England and the Colonies.[5]

Draw your own conclusions about the impact of ten million or more teachers trained in this fashion. I believe the consequences were devastating for our primary educational systems (K–12), but for our colleges and universities they have been catastrophic. Academia has been the primary source for "what we know that isn't so."

Dr. Max Rafferty, former head of the California school system and controversial author of *Suffer, Little Children,* offers a scathing commentary on American education:

> The great wheel of history has turned ponderously full-circle since the Punic Wars. A happier time for children dawned a century ago, and in that Golden Age, a whole new pantheon of youthful gods and goddesses came down from Mount Olympus and made old earth a magic place for boys and girls.
>
> Wilfred of Ivanhoe rose stirrup to stirrup with Coeur de Leon and the evil hold of Torquilstone burned eternal witness to the power of youth and goodness. Laughing and shouting in the same great company rose Arthur with his Round Table, forever splintering their lances in the cause of right . . . roistering and invincible swaggered Porthos, Athos, and Aramis, with the young D'Artagnan, ever ready

to draw those magic blades, the wonder of the world, for truth and glory and the queen. The horn of Roland echoed through the pass at Roncesvalles.

Were not these fit gods for the children of mankind? Apart and in a merry company leaped and played the Child Immortals. Hand in hand the long haired Alice walked with Christopher Robin, bright eyes alert for talking to rabbits and greedy little bears. Sturdy Jim Hawkins counted his pieces of eight . . . While young Tom Sawyer kept a wary lookout for the menace that was Injun Joe.

When in any age have children had such shining exemplars?

Hansel and Gretel have been dehydrated and neutralized to the status of Cincinnati children on a Sunday-school picnic, and Jack the Giant-Killer to a schoolboy swatting flies. Everything that was fearful and wonderful and glamorous has been leveled off to the lowest common denominator.

Ulysses and Penelope have been replaced by Dick and Jane in the textbooks of our schools. The quest for the Golden Fleece has been crowded by the visit of Tom and Susan to the zoo. Jackie pursues his insipid goal of a ride in the district garbage truck with good, old crotchety Mr. Jones, while the deathless ride of Paul Revere goes unsung, unhonored and unwept. It is interesting, and certainly significant, that modern education has deliberately debunked the hero to make room for the jerk. The lofty exception to the rank and file, whom all of us could envy and emulate, has been compelled to give way to the Great Mediocrity, and the synthesis of all that is harmless and safe and banal among us.

Watch the abler ones grow dull and apathetic, bored and lackluster, as they yawn and watch the clock over the stupid adventures of Muk-Muk the Eskimo Boy, or little Pedro from Argentina. Then, suddenly, as though opening an enchanted window upon a radiant pageant, give them the story of the wrath of Achilles. Let them stand with Casabianca upon the burning deck. Trek with them in spirit to the Yukon, and ... Place them upon the shot-swept shrouds of Bonhomme Richard, and let them thrill to those words flashing like a rapier out of the past, "I have not yet begun to fight." Kneel with them behind the cotton bales at New Orleans with Andy Jackson at their side as the redcoats begin to emerge from the mist of the Louisiana swamps, and the sullen guns of LaFitte begin to pound. Watch their faces.[6]

True, the sudden and unexpected appearance of Sputnik I in 1957 shook the educational world to its shoelaces and gave rise to major re-evaluations which discarded much of the detritus of progressive education. Nevertheless, much of its philosophy will remain until three or more generations have phased out the last of its effects. Meanwhile, the federal government is stepping into the educational arena through Federal Aid to Education. Who pays the piper calls the tune. As the U.S. Supreme Court stated in *Wickard v. Filburn* (October 1942), "It is hardly lack of due process for the government to regulate that which it subsidizes ..."

No doubt many Americans were surprised by that decision, having failed to realize that they could not simultaneously accept federal subsidies and retain local control of their schools.

Those responsible for omitting or misinterpreting the history of this country at the K–12 levels have indirectly created a major threat to the survival of a free and ordered society. Most teachers are dedicated people who cannot be faulted for what they were not taught. To what extent this lack of knowledge explains the frequently intransigent behavior of their union leadership is yet to be determined. In any event, ideas totally antithetical to the principles upon which this Republic was founded have found their way into the halls of higher education and have taken control of the philosophical heart of many colleges and universities.

Dr. George Roche, the highly respected president of Hillsdale College, says ruefully, "All too many of our colleges and

universities are academically, morally, spiritually, and financially bankrupt."

In the introduction to his most recent book, *The Fall of the
Ivory Tower*, he says:

> Higher education in America has become a popular
> bull's-eye, and with good reason. In spite of a massive
> infusion of money, including federal aid, which has dou-
> bled over the last few years, tens of thousands of students
> do not know when Columbus sailed to the New World, who
> wrote the Declaration of Independence, or when the Civil
> War was fought. Businesses complain that they must
> reeducate college graduates in such basic subjects as gram-
> mar, spelling, and practical math. Parents protest that
> tuition costs have far outstripped the rate of inflation and
> their ability to pay. Meanwhile, growing numbers of pro-
> fessors receive huge salaries for teaching one or two classes
> a semester. Though constantly complaining about a lack
> of sufficient research opportunities and funds, they, as
> well as many administrators, have found ample time
> and resources to politicize the campus and to lead a
> frontal assault on the traditional liberal arts curriculum
> all under the banners of "political correctness" and "mul-
> ticulturalism."[7]

Why has this happened? Scores of books and articles assert
that the primary explanation is the takeover, in the 1980s and
early 1990s, of the high-education establishment by the political and intellectual radicals of the 1960s. Once in power, these
teachers clothed their liberal-left agenda on race, class, and
gender in the mantle of diversity, in much the same way that
the troops in Desert Storm camouflaged their tanks with net-
ting. Thus concealed, the diversity troops launched an all-out
campaign to displace traditional values and academic disci-
plines. And they have enjoyed great success. The intellectual
revolution they fomented on campuses is one of the most critical events of our time. Like the academic ills it has encouraged,

however, it is actually a consequence of something else. That something else is government. At one time the dominant form of education in this country was private, but now the government controls most of our schools and the effect of federal subsidy and control has been more profound, more direct, and more damaging that anyone realized. The entire system of American higher education is going academically, morally, and literally bankrupt.

Student loan assistance at the federal level alone costs the taxpayers $22 billion annually. Add state aid and other related sources and our tax bill hits $38 billion annually. The default rate on these loans is running at 30 percent; Pell Grants, a federal program designed to help needy students, has been so seriously corrupted that, in New York State alone, some 34 percent of the funds have gone to nonexistent institutions and students.

More than 75 percent of the funding of our institutions of higher learning comes from the federal government, approximately 15 percent from tuition, and the balance from private and corporate generosity. Even so, more colleges and universities than ever before are in financial crisis.

The Department of Education intrudes increasingly into colleges and universities, attempting to reshape higher education. By mandating the lowering of academic standards and exploiting the power of accreditation, the D.O.E. has pushed America's prestigious institutions to the brink of academic and financial collapse. Meanwhile, tuitions have increased at three times the rate of inflation, and some of the added costs must be laid at the door of government regulations.

Even at such supposedly elite institutions as Yale, Harvard, the University of Michigan, UCLA, Dartmouth, and Stanford, core curriculums have been decimated. Scores of graduates write at a junior-high-school level, and general educational quality has dropped significantly.

The statistics are indeed discouraging. Fifty percent of the student body never graduate; roughly 25 percent take six years or more to complete their studies; and at least 50 percent are unable to perform at an acceptable level in the business world.[8] If you have children nearing college age, I recommend Dr. Roche's treatise (see endnotes) as an aid in selecting a school. To what degree these problems arise from conspiracy, ignorance, or ineptitude would be difficult to say. But the consequences of these educational deficiencies are apparent: government grows ever more intrusive; society is wreaked with accelerating violence; and our cultural values are weakening.

There is another contributor to the accelerated growth of centralized government, and it may be the most significant of all—though it would not exist without the catalysts we have already discussed. Once a government has seized or been granted the power to tax all forms of income (wages, interest, dividends from investments, capital gains, etc.) and has established graduated rates—the highest of which are levied on those who contribute the most—the transfer society is in place. In a transfer society, income and wealth are redistributed on a massive scale with the goal of leveling everyone. Politicians in such a society purchase permanent power by giving what Citizen A has earned to Citizen B, who will then vote to sustain the politicians' power.

Notes

1. Dean Russell, *Freedom Follows the Free Market* (Irvington-on-Hudson, N.Y.: Foundation for Economic Education, 1963).
2. Norman Thomas, Address to the Young Presidents' Club, Drake Hotel, Chicago, 1961.
3. Martin Gross, *Government Racket: Washington Waste from A to Z* (New York: Bantam, 1992).
4. Allan H. Meltzer, *Why Government Grows* (Ottawa, Ill.: Green Hill Publications, 1976).
5. Augustin Rudd, *Bending of the Twig* (Chicago: Heritage Press, 1957).
6. Max Rafferty, *Suffer, Little Children* (New York: Devon-Adair Company, 1962).
7. George Roche, *The Fall of the Ivory Tower: Government Funding, Corruption, and the Bankrupting of American Higher Education* (Washington, D.C.: Regnery-Gateway, 1994).
8. Ibid.

CHAPTER SEVEN

The Transfer Society

Frederic Bastiat (1801–1850) was a French economist, statesman, and author who wrote both before and immediately after France's February Revolution of 1848. At that time France was turning inexorably toward socialism.

Bastiat's treatise *The Law*, published in 1850, is only seventy-five pages long and was written over 145 years ago. Nevertheless, it is among the finest existing expositions on human liberty, filled with devastating perceptions that might have been written yesterday.

What Is Law?
What then is the law? It is the collective organization of the individual right to lawful defense. If every person has the right to defend—even by force—his person, his liberty, and his property, then it follows that a group of men have the right to organize and support a common force to protect these rights constantly. Thus, since an individual cannot lawfully use force against the person, liberty, or property of another individual, the common force—for the same reason—cannot lawfully be used to destroy the person, liberty, or property of individuals or groups.

How to Identify Legal Plunder

But how is this legal plunder to be identified? Quite simply. See if the law takes from some persons what belongs to them, and gives it to other persons to whom it does not belong. See if the law benefits one citizen at the expense of another by doing what the citizen himself cannot do without committing a crime. Then abolish this law without delay, for it is not only an evil itself, but also it is a fertile source for further evil because it invites reprisals.

The Choice Before Us

The question of legal plunder must be settled once and for all, and there are only three ways to settle it:

1. The few plunder the many.
2. Everybody plunders everybody.
3. Nobody plunders anybody.

We must make our choice among limited plunder, universal plunder, and no plunder. The law can follow only one of these three.

A Just and Enduring Government

If a nation is founded on the basis that nobody plunders anybody, it seems to me that order would prevail among the people, in thought as well as in deed. It seems to me that such a nation would have the most simple, easy to accept, economical, limited, non-oppressive, just and enduring government imaginable—whatever its political form might be.

Under such an administration, everyone would understand that he possessed all the privileges as well as all the responsibilities of his existence. No one would have any argument with government, provided that his person was respected, his labor was free, and the fruits of his labor were protected against all unjust attack. When successful, we would not have to thank the state for our success. And, conversely, when unsuccessful, we would no more think of blaming the state for our misfortune than would the farmers blame the state because of hail or frost. The state would be felt only by the invaluable blessings of safety provided by this concept of government.

A Fatal Tendency of Mankind

But there is another tendency that is common among people. When they can, they wish to live and prosper at the expense of others. This is no rash accusation. Nor does it come from a gloomy and uncharitable spirit. The annals of history bear witness to the truth of it: incessant wars, mass migrations, religious persecutions, universal slavery, dishonesty in commerce, and monopolies. This fatal desire has its origin in the very nature of man—in that primitive, universal and insuppressible instinct that impels him to satisfy his desires with the least possible pain.

Property and Plunder

Man can live and satisfy his wants only by ceaseless labor; by the ceaseless application of his faculties to natural resources. This process is the origin of property. But it is also true that a man may live and satisfy his wants by seizing and consuming the products of the labor of others. This process is the origin of plunder. When, then does plunder stop? It stops when it becomes more painful and more dangerous than labor.

The Seductive Lure of Socialism

Here I encounter the most popular fallacy of our times. It is not considered sufficient that the law should be just; it must be philanthropic. Nor is it sufficient that the law should guarantee every citizen the free and inoffensive use of his faculties for physical, intellectual, and moral self-improvement. Instead, it is demanded that the law should directly extend welfare, education, and morality throughout the nation.[1]

The Growth of a Transfer Society

With Bastiat's observations in mind, let us consider the evolution of a transfer society. In its first stage, the society accepts the idea that it is proper for government to take from the rich and give to the poor. The initial question, then, becomes, Who is rich?

The Tax Foundation, a non-profit research organization, reports that in 1987 there were 36,299 people with annual adjusted gross incomes of one million dollars or more. If they were taxed at the rate of 100 percent, the government could run for exactly sixteen days. There simply are not enough millionaires to pay the full freight. What if we expand our definition of rich to include everyone with a taxable annual income of $500,000 or more? If the 113, 390 individuals who filed at that level in 1987 were taxed at 100 percent, the government could run for twenty-seven days. So let's tax at 100 percent everyone with an adjusted gross income above $200,000. In 1987 there were 545,177 of them—enough to fund the government for a full six weeks.[2]

This first stage of the transfer society in the United States was launched in the 1930s, and for practical purposes it ran out of gas before 1959, because the rich were taxed to the limit.

At the second stage, the transfer society goes after the income of the middle class and increases taxes while instigating deficit spending. The resulting inflation collapses the value of savings and investments. At the end of stage two, debtors are gaining and creditors are losing. (By way of example, remember that in the 1970s, the savings of all Americans were eroded by 60 percent because of inflation, and the most drastic effects were visited on the middle class.)

The United States entered the second stage in the early 1960s and moved rapidly to the third stage. *Now it is not the rich who carry the bulk of the tax burden, but the 90 percent or so of American workers who earn between $30,000 and $80,000.* Thus, society starts living off the efforts and savings of the middle class, who must support massive programs—many of them designed to benefit the poor. Some seventy-nine separate and overlapping welfare programs cost roughly $320 billion in 1995, more than was spent on defense. In fact the cost of welfare alone increased almost 800 percent between 1965 and 1992.

During those years, welfare spending (federal, state, and local) cost the American taxpayer $5 trillion, more than it cost to win World War II, *even in constant, inflation-adjusted dollars.*[3]

Walter Williams says:

> With 5 trillion dollars, you could purchase every factory in the U.S., all manufacturing equipment and every office building. With what's left over, you could buy every airline, trucking company and our commercial maritime fleet. If you're still in the shopping mood, you could also buy every television, radio and power company, plus every retail and wholesale store in the nation.
>
> In order to finance the welfare agenda, Congress forces each tax-paying household to pay $3,400 per year in taxes. If the definition of slavery is, "one person being forcibly used to serve the purposes of another," then slavery is the essence of the program.

A recent Cato Institute study focuses on six of the most common types of welfare assistance—AFDC, food stamps, Medicaid, housing, nutrition assistance, and energy assistance. On a state-by-state basis, the Cato study calculated the value of this six-piece welfare package for a welfare mother with two children. The value ranged from a high of $36,400 in Hawaii to a low of $11,500 in Mississippi. In sixteen states and the District of Columbia, the welfare package was more generous than a ten-dollar-an-hour job. It paid, in effect, 2½ times the minimum wage because these benefits *are not taxed.*

It is stunningly unfair that millions of hard-working, moderate-income families are paying taxes to support a public assistance system that provides a higher living standard than they have achieved by working. In four states, the average worker receives less compensation after taxes than the average welfare recipient.

Even the definition of "poor" raises serious questions. To most Americans, poverty means destitution—the inability to provide one's family with food, clothing, and shelter. Robert Rector, senior policy analyst of The Heritage Foundation, who is widely considered the most knowledgeable authority on the subject, has researched this issue thoroughly. Some of his findings:

1. Nearly 40 percent of the poor own their own homes.
2. More than three quarters of a million poor persons own homes worth over $100,000; 71,000 own homes worth over $300,000.
3. The average poor American has twice as much living space as the average non-poor Japanese and four times as much as the average non-poor Russian.
4. 91 percent of poor households have color televisions; 29 percent have two or more.
5. Nearly 60 percent of poor households have air conditioning.
6. 65 percent of poor households have a car; 14 percent have two or more cars.
7. 56 percent of poor households own microwave ovens.
8. Close to 25 percent of poor households have automatic dishwashers, and nearly 33 percent have stand-alone freezers in addition to their refrigerators.[4]

Not only are the definitions used in welfare legislation questionable, some of its programs also border on lunacy. If a teenaged girl would like to get out from under her parents' jurisdiction, all she has to do is engage in premarital sex, get pregnant, drop out of high school, and bear the child without getting married. Then she will be paid about $800 a month (tax free). Is it any surprise that between 1960 and 1990, the illegitimacy rate among low-income whites rose from 2.3 percent to 21 percent? Among blacks, it went from 23 percent to 65 percent.

Such numbers disturbed many legislators, even in the liberal camp, and in 1996 President Clinton finally (after vetoing two earlier versions) signed the Welfare Reform Bill passed by the 104th Congress. This bill will alleviate some of the current problems, but it will take several years for the effects of reform to be felt.

Meanwhile, what about, for example, Medicaid? When the program was proposed in 1965, it was projected to cost about a billion dollars a year by 1990. By 1991 the actual cost was $56 billion—a 5,500 percent increase. (Medicare costs were estimated to reach $9 to $12 billion by 1990, but the actual cost was $107 billion—a leap of approximately 1,000 percent! So much for government estimates.)[5]

What the government identifies as transfer payments— e.g., Social Security, welfare programs, Medicare, and Medicaid—are generally referred to as entitlements and involve the direct transfer of funds collected from taxpayers to specific groups of recipients. In fact, transfer payments are involved in almost every area of government activity. Under the departments of Health and Human Services as well as Agriculture, Commerce, Energy, and others, the same essential function is being carried out either directly or indirectly.

Entitlements have achieved the status of a new art form, not only by transferring the earnings of taxpayers in a given fiscal year, but also by passing on a massive debt to future generations. At the current rate, a child born today will have to pay $185,000 in taxes during his or her lifetime just to cover the *interest* on the debt.

In *The Communist Manifesto* by Karl Marx and Friedrich Engels (1848) Marx ponders the methods by which a free (capitalist) society can be destroyed to make room for a regimented (communist) one:

We have seen above that the first step in the revolution by the working class is to raise the proletariat to the position of ruling class, to win the battle of democracy.

The proletariat will use its political supremacy to wrest, by degrees, all capital from the bourgeoisie, to centralize all instruments of production in the hands of the State, i.e. of the proletariat organized as the ruling class; and to increase the total production forces as rapidly as possible.

Of course, in the beginning, this cannot be affected except by means of despotic inroads on the right of property, and on conditions of bourgeois production, by means of measures, therefore, which appear untenable, but which, in the course of the movement, outstrip themselves, necessitate further inroads upon the old social order, and are unavoidable as a means of entirely revolutionizing the mode of production.

These measures will, of course, be different in different countries. Nevertheless, in the most advanced countries, the following will be pretty generally applicable.

1. Abolition of property in land and application of all rents of land to public purposes.
2. A heavy progressive or graduated income tax.
3. Abolition of all right of inheritance.
4. Confiscation of the property of all emigrants and rebels.
5. Centralization of credit in the hands of the State, by means of a national bank with State capital and exclusive monopoly.
6. Centralization of the means of communication and transport in the hands of the State.
7. Extension of factories and instruments of production owned by the State, and bringing into cultivation of waste lands, and the improvement of the soil generally in accordance with a common plan.
8. Equal liability of all labor. Establishment of industrial armies, especially for agriculture.

9. Combination of agriculture with manufacturing industries; gradual abolition of the distinction between town and country.

10. Free education for all children in public schools. Abolition of children's factory in its present form. Combination of education with industrial production.[6]

The Fallout from a Transfer Society

There are other aspects of the transfer society that deserve some attention. For instance, there are some 1,250+ advisory boards, panels, councils, commissions, and committees under federal jurisdiction. (No one knows exactly how many.) Take a look at your tax dollars at work. You support advisory panels on: Anthropology, Astronomy, Dance, Drama, Folk Music and Jazz, Academic Music, Coins and Medals, Expansion Arts, Dental Devices, and Hemorrhoidal Drugs, to name a few.

You pay the costs of advisory committees for: Radiation Biology Aspect of the SST, San Jose Mission Historic Site, Alcohol Training Review, Career Development, Epilepsy, Fine Arts, Peanuts, Raisins, Waterfowl, Recovery of Archaeological Remains, Laxatives, Social Problems, Theater, and Contraceptives, among others.

You sponsor advisory boards for Promotion of Rifle Practice, Tea Experts, Alcoholism, Oral Biology, Hematology, Nephology, North Kaibab Grazing, Outer Planets, Peach Sales, Pear Sales, Wolf Trap Farm Park, Plant Variety, Fremont National Forest Grazing, and many, many more.

You cover the expenses of advisory councils for: National Arboretum, National Archives, National Cotton, Indian Opportunity, Quality of Education, Arts, Humanities, Ethnic Heritage, Indian Education, Nurse Training, Drug Abuse, and several other topics. Through these boards, etc., you have given:

1. $17,000 to the Bedouins for a dry-cleaning plant
2. $70,000 for a study of the perspiration of Australian aborigines

3. $15,000 to scientists who wished to study Yugoslavian lizards
4. $71,000 for scholars to compile a history of comic books
5. $5,000 for an analysis of violin varnish
6. $19,300 to determine why children fall off bicycles
7. $375,000 to the Pentagon for a study of frisbees[7]

But wait—there's more! The transfer society also contributes to what is generally referred to as the "pork barrel." The House of Representatives essentially controls the purse strings of the nation, and its members are sometimes afflicted with an overwhelming desire to "bring home the bacon" to their states or districts. The practice of "you-vote-for-my-pet-project-and-I'll-vote-for-yours" keeps the pork barrel costing billions of dollars every year. There are, of course, appropriate government projects in the mix, but you can also find:

$6.4 million for a Bavarian ski resort in Kellogg, Idaho
$13 million to repair a privately owned dam in South Dakota
$3.1 million to convert a ferry boat into a crab restaurant
$43 million to recreate a railroad yard of old in Pennsylvania
$4.3 million for a private museum in Johnstown, Pennsylvania
$11 million for a private pleasure boat harbor in Cleveland
$6 million to repair tracks owned by the Soo Railroad Line
$2.7 million for a catfish farm in Arkansas
$19 million to examine gas emissions from cow flatulence
$10 million for an access ramp in a Milwaukee stadium
$500 thousand to build a replica of the Great Pyramid in Indiana
$3 million for private parking garages in Chicago
$20 million for a demonstration project on wooden bridges

$33 million to pump sand into private beaches in Miami[8]

And this is a very short list. These items are minor expenditures compared to some bills your taxes are paying. For instance, have you ever heard of the D.C. Air Force? Our government owns twelve thousand military aircraft and leases another five thousand every year. This fleet is operated and maintained by six thousand employees. How necessary do you supposed this major expense is? At least $1.7 billion a year could be saved without sacrificing any significant transportation capability.

Staff expansion is another staggering expense. In the early 1960s, 700 committee staff members served the House and Senate. Today—and remember that we still have the same number of representatives and senators—there are 3,700 staff members (a fivefold increase in thirty years). If we trimmed these staffs we could save about $250 million a year.

Each member of the House and Senate also has his or her own office staff. That's an additional 16,000 employees. During the Truman administration each member had five aides, for a total of 2,825 staffers.

Referring back to our discussion of property, you may find it interesting that the federal government is by far the nation's largest landowner, claiming some 700 billion acres, over one third of our total land mass. (Government lands are equal in size to all of the states west of the Rockies.) In fact, the government owns 86 percent of Nevada and 60 percent of California.

The four agencies with land ownership—the National Forest Service, the Department of the Interior, the National Park Service, and the Fish and Wildlife Service—continue to purchase land and to pay extravagant prices for it. At present they budget $135 million a year for such purchases. (If they sold 250 billion acres—a little more than a third of their holdings—at $2,000 per acre, the $5 trillion would come close to paying off our national debt.)[9]

Obviously, the federal government has not just strayed from the principles expressed in our Declaration of Independence and Constitution, it has gone into orbit. Neither fiscal sanity nor common sense is evident in most of its operations. Back in February of 1982, President Reagan announced the formation of the President's Private Sector Survey on Cost Control with J. Peter Grace as chairman.

The Grace Commission consisted of 36 task forces chaired by 161 top individuals from the corporate, academic, and labor spheres. It was staffed by 2,000 talented individuals. Eighteen months later, after a rigorous evaluation of the bureaucracy, the commission published its findings.

In 36 major reports and 11 special subject studies, commission members indicated that the federal budget could be slashed by $424 billion over a three-year period by eliminating unchallenged waste.[10] President Reagan implemented as many of the commission's suggestions as he could by executive order, but Congress balked where its cooperation was required.

Clearly, then, our economic and personal liberties are being drastically eroded. The potential consequences of this development are dire, and apathy is a luxury we cannot afford.[11]

Notes

1. Bastiat, *The Law*.
2. Tax Foundation, *Reader's Digest* (May 1994).
3. Robert Rector, *How the Poor Really Live* (Washington, D.C.: The Heritage Foundation, 1993).
4. Ibid.
5. Ibid.
6. Samuel Moore, *The Communist Manifesto* (Washington, D.C.: Regnery, 1954).
7. Donald Lambro, *The Federal Rathole* (New Rochelle, N.Y.: Arlington House, 1975).
8. Gross, *Government Racket*.
9. Ibid.
10. R. W. Lee and W. R. Kennedy, *The Grace Commission Report* (Ottawa, Ill.: Jameson Books, 1984).
11. All statistics quoted here have been rechecked where possible in *Budget of the U.S. Government, 1993* or *Statistical Abstract of the United States, 1993*.

CHAPTER EIGHT

———

Our Cultural Collapse

A long with the undermining of our property rights and the incursions into our individual liberties, we have suffered serious attacks on our cultural values. Indeed, ours has become the most violent society in the industrialized world. Turn on the evening news. You'll watch a virtual parade of rapes, murders, drive-by shootings, carjackings, and other acts of violence. In city after city, civil order is only precipitously maintained. *"Domestic tranquility"* is a quaint concept on streets ruled by teenaged gangs. Mothers are shot trying to protect their children on the street—and even in their very homes—from drive-by shooters. Drugs are sold on street corners, and in too many school corridors knifings are common occurrences.

The stunning statistics understate the tragedy. Los Angeles alone reportedly harbors more than 200,000 armed and organized gang members, and Chicago is home to 165,000 more. Every year in the United States, 23,000 citizens are murdered. Over six million additional violent crimes (rapes, assaults, and robberies) are committed every year. According to the FBI, the number of violent crimes reported to police has skyrocketed from 168 per 100,000 people in 1963 to 758 per 100,000 people today. In the last three to five years, crime rates have begun to decline, but the numbers remain appalling, and a climate of fear pervades our cities.

In 1991, 1.2 million children (almost 30 percent of all births) were born to unmarried mothers, and in many inner cities the figure approaches 80 percent. What's more, the Guttmacher Institute reports that over three million American teenagers—one out of every eight—acquire a sexually transmitted disease. America now "boasts" the highest rates of teen pregnancy, abortion, and illegitimate childbirth in the industrialized world.

When these problems attracted public attention, the government stepped forward with its usual solution: money. A bevy of agencies threw every dollar they could raise at the dilemma. The worse the situation became, the more they spent; and the more they spent, the worse the situation became. To date, federal spending on social programs has amounted to $5 trillion, and the social pathologies continue to grow.

When the mayor of a major American city was asked privately about the gang problem, he replied that the city was helpless to control the more than 100,000 gang members: "As a result of the drug trade, the gangs have more money than we do—they have more guns than we do—and they have better lawyers than we do." Asked whether the National Guard or some other military force might be able forcibly to confiscate illegal firearms and arrest their owners, he nodded. "We probably could. But if we did we would be in litigation with the ACLU for the next twenty years—and we simply couldn't afford it." (Personally, I'd be happy to see my tax dollars used to argue the city's case.)

Crime, of course, is not the only problem. Television talk shows are carnivals featuring everything from transvestites and wife-beaters to gay rights activists and grave robbers. Television movies portray excessive violence and deplorable behavior of all kinds, urging on young, impressionable, inexperienced, and yet-to-be-educated minds the idea that such behavior is both normal and acceptable.

The Hollywood elite who produce, direct, and perform in most major entertainments are unaware of, or unconcerned with, or downright hostile to traditional values. Oliver Stone, director of *JFK, Wall Street,* and *Born on the Fourth of July,* was questioned about the overwhelming preoccupation with sex and violence that permeates Hollywood. He replied, "Anything goes . . . . Artistic merit is more important than content." Unfortunately, if an immature and uneducated mind is put on a movie diet of *Basic Instinct, Fatal Attraction, Total Recall,* and *Silence of the Lambs,* with MTV, "Beavis and Butthead," and Madonna for dessert, society should expect some psychological indigestion. To quote the late Chicago *Tribune* columnist Mike Royko, "I enjoy trash as much as the next guy—but the quality of the trash has declined precipitously."

Some defenders of Hollywood maintain that the entertainment industry just gives the public what it wants, but movie attendance has dropped since 1984 to a two-movie-per-year average in 1994. In addition, many films preoccupied with sex, violence, or both have lost money—though teenaged attendance at questionable films remains high.

John Underwood put it well: "In a society where anything goes, everything eventually will."

From sex and violence it was a short journey to open ridicule and hateful treatment of religion, especially the more traditional Protestant and Catholic faiths. Now, our freedoms guarantee everyone the right to reject the values of most of our society, but must we allow attacks on the basic values of most Americans over the public air waves? To be consistent with our principles, we must take individual responsibility for responding to these attacks rather than demand that government censors respond for us.

Our welfare system did in fact grow out of good intentions, but its fallout has caused a shift in public attitudes, especially those of young people. To quote social scientist James Q. Wilson, "Our young people have been encouraged to embrace an ethos that values self-expression over self-control."

The justice system, too, is faltering for want of common sense. A judge in Shreveport, Louisiana, recently ruled that the teaching of abstinence may not be included in a sex-education program for high school students. Abstinence, said the judge, is a religiously based virtue, and to teach it in the public schools is to violate the separation of church and state.

No wonder many people are angry and frustrated to discover that they are held hostage by an arrogant group of contemptuous intellectuals with little use for the institutions that have provided our moral foundations: the family and the church. Worse, such thinking seems to pervade our education system at all levels, to infiltrate the halls of government, and to permeate the electronic and print media.

The cultural effects are measurable. Under the auspices of The Heritage Foundation, William Bennett compiled the *Index of Leading Cultural Indicators*. Drawn from unimpeachable sources, it documents our cultural crisis in several areas:

Crime While the population has increased only 41 percent since 1960, violent crime has increased 560 percent and total crime by over 300 percent. The fastest growing segment of the criminal population is made up of children between the ages of ten and seventeen. Eight of every ten Americans can expect to be a victim of crime at least once.

Poverty More than one child in eight comes under the AFDC (Aid to Families with Dependent Children) program. Twelve percent of children under the age of six who live with married parents live in poverty. Of those who live with only their mothers, 66 percent live in poverty.

Family Teenage pregnancy has nearly doubled in the past two decades. The percentage of out-of-wedlock births has gone from 5 percent in 1960 to 29 percent in 1993.

The percentage of children living in single-parent homes has more than tripled in the past three decades. Since 1960 the teen suicide rate has more than tripled. Tragically, more than 5 percent of U.S. teenagers attempted suicide in 1990.

Education   Since 1960, the constant dollars spent per student have almost tripled to $6,000. Meanwhile, SAT scores have tumbled more than 80 points.[1]

It seems glaringly obvious that the more our government taxes and spends at all levels, the worse our problems become. Virtue and self-discipline were crucial to our nation's founding, and they are no less crucial to its survival.

Notes
1. Bennett, *Index.*

CHAPTER NINE

The American Economic Miracle

W ise though they were, the founding fathers could not have foreseen the economic miracle produced by an environment of individual liberty. When the Age of Capitalism dawned in the 1800s, it had been preceded by one command system after another:

> The Age of Military Socialism 300–500 AD
> The Age of Feudalism 500–1500 AD
> The Age of Mercantilism 1500–1800 AD

Until very recently in world history the majority of people were, economically, serfs. But for Adam Smith, Jeremy Bentham, David Hume, John Locke and their colleagues, most of us would still be serfs.

How did our nation, in the course of its short history, create a society in which a family of modest means has access to a cornucopia of foods and an abundance of gadgets for preparing them, a dazzling array of entertainments and of electronic machinery to bring it into the home, affordable clothing, air-conditioned homes and workplaces, medicine chests filled with lifesaving or pain-relieving drugs, automobiles, personal computers, etc.? The average American consumes twice as many goods and services today as twenty years ago, and in 1947 we thought we were enjoying an unprecedented standard of living.[1]

And we were. Even in 1947, before massive increases in imports, Americans owned:

- 85% of the world's automobiles
- 60% of the world's life insurance policies
- 54% of the world's telephones
- 48% of the world's radio sets
- 46% of the world's electric power capacity
- 92% of the world's modern bathtubs

Even earlier—prior to World War II—Americans consumed:

- 60% of the world's rubber
- 50% of the world's coffee
- 40% of the world's salt[2]

Yet, despite our resounding successes in these areas, Americans have amazingly little collective knowledge of the history and functioning of commerce and industry. We either *don't know* or *know what isn't so* about American business because, in the words of Nazi Propaganda Minister Joseph Goebbels, "If you tell a big lie often enough it soon becomes a fact of history."

Big Business—Bad Business??

How has the American business community been portrayed in our public school systems, our colleges and universities, our news media, and our entertainment (television shows and movies)?

I suggest that throughout your school years, your history textbooks and most of your teachers emphasized that the nineteenth century in the United States was a time of unrestrained individualism exploited by heartless capitalists who virtually enslaved their workers in the name of profit. The rich got richer at the expense of the poor and the downtrodden.

In fact, the nineteenth century *was* a period of rugged individualism, and it did produce some rapacious entrepreneurs.

But at no other period in human history did the ordinary working man experience such unprecedented improvement in his standard of living as he did between 1865 and 1920. The evidence is incontrovertible, supported by economic statistics showing the dramatic rise in national income and by the tidal wave of immigrants that washed over the United States during that period. Clearly, people did not immigrate to this country in overcrowded ships over often stormy seas to be worse off. The most emphatic way people can vote is with their feet.

Indeed, this period of alleged heartless capitalist cruelty was actually a time of immense generosity and charity. The first nonprofit hospitals and libraries were established, and scores of colleges and universities were founded.

Nevertheless, the academic elite and the media (most of whom have *no* knowledge of manufacturing or commerce) portray business as corrupt and amoral, allowing a few greedy individuals to profited at the expense of the broader community. Both on television and in the movies, business executives are increasingly the villains, selling shoddy and overpriced products and/or endangering the health of their workers and neighbors to make a quick buck. By the 1970s, the revisionist history of business had become a flood of criticism, hostility, and misinformation.

Our commerce is based on the principle of willing exchange. If you purchase a car for $18,000, it is because you prefer having the car to keeping your money, and the seller prefers having your money to keeping the car in his inventory. If the car dealer is charging too much—i.e., if the car in question is not worth $18,000 to you—you will look elsewhere. You have choices. You are not forced to buy the overpriced car because it's the only one for sale or because there is a long waiting list for cars coming from a government factory. Thus, in a free market the business community cannot force you to buy anything. The government has a monopoly on the legal use of force.

Back in the early 1900s the United States began moving gradually from a free and open economy to a mixed system, combining elements of a free market with government intervention in the form of regulations—some justified, many unnecessary and excessive.

Let's stop here for a few definitions, to put American business in perspective:

Businesses exist to produce and sell products and services. They respond to and thrive on competition, price fluctuations, freely negotiated contracts, optimism, and the ongoing search for innovation and efficiency.

Governments exist to protect people and extract revenue from people. They thrive on a monopoly of sovereignty and authority, on supplying services to all.

Charities exist to give things away. They thrive on cooperation, gifts, volunteerism, services, altruism or religious values, compassion, and enlightenment.[3]

The adjective *big* is attached to the noun *business* as if they were Siamese twins. In fact, less than 1 percent of U.S. corporations providing goods and/or services have more than five hundred employees; approximately 95 percent have fewer than one hundred employees; and roughly 31 percent have fewer than twenty employees. There are also vast numbers of unincorporated businesses, including 32 million home-based businesses and sole-proprietorships. What's more, big businesses (500+ employees) employ less than 20 percent of America's work force, and less than 5 percent of America's wealth is held by manufacturing corporations with assets of one billion dollars or more. In terms of GNP (gross national product), corporations provide 60 percent, other businesses 25 percent, and non-profit corporations and household enterprises account for the remaining 15 percent.[4] So much for the dominance of big business.

Business is the primary source of all wealth, all taxes, and all economic growth. If there were no employers, there would be no employees. Government has no wealth other than what it takes from the profits of business and from the wages and salaries of those who work and produce. That wealth is taken in the form of taxes as well as through inflation, regulatory costs, and government debt. To strangle a business with confiscatory taxes is to kill the goose that lays the golden egg. Although big businesses are less prevalent than the current myths would suggest, it is worth considering where they come from. They are not born full grown, ready to snuff out smaller competitors and run roughshod over consumers. Most businesses start out very small: John Hertz's little car-rental lot in Chicago; Roland Macy's dry-goods store in New York; even engine-maker Mott and wheelwright Durant's little shop—which grew up to be General Motors. Similarly, the Ford Motor Company, Minnesota Mining and Manufacturing (3M), and most others started very small. They became big businesses because the public bought their products. It is true, of course, that industries like steel and petroleum require large capital investment from the beginning, but they are the exception rather than the rule.

The few companies that do become large generate thousands of small companies. For example, 3M uses products and services from more than thirty thousand small businesses; Hewlett-Packard deals with more than six thousand small companies; and Caterpillar, General Motors, General Electric, Xerox, and IBM function in precisely the same way, providing (directly or indirectly) millions of jobs for American workers.

When the automobile was first produced only the very wealthy could afford it. It was the ingenuity of American producers that made it possible to produce cars for the mass market. It was Henry Ford who determined that his workers should be able to buy the cars they manufactured. He devised a more efficient process, got his costs down, and achieved that goal. Even such a simple item as women's hosiery was originally created for the "wealthy few," but today it's on the legs of almost every woman in America, not a luxury but an everyday necessity.

What about the much-discussed "power of the big corporations." Of course, a corporation has power, but what can a corporation force you to do? A government, on the other hand, can deprive you of your life, your liberty, or your property. It can arrest you, put you in jail, take your money by force, or inflate the currency so that your money is all but worthless.

As for monopolies, how many texts or teachers point out that government influence and power are essential to sustain a monopoly? The free and competitive market will always control commerce unless government regulations or subsidies are injected, as they are in the cases of transportation, communications, and energy—all of which are regulated to "help consumers" (apparently by saving them the trouble of choosing for themselves). For a penetrating examination of how "most government bureaus and regulatory agencies tend to accomplish precisely the reverse of their original intentions," read Milton Friedman's *Capitalism and Freedom.*

Another myth from the *what we know that isn't so* category concerns the function of profits. The sources referred to earlier (academia, the media, etc.) have given profits a bad reputation. To the untutored, profits are "bad" and high profits are "unconscionable and contrary to the best interests of the working class and the consumer." Nothing could be further from the truth. Even the term "working class" is freighted. It is used to describe those who work on the plant floor, behind the store counter, in the steno pool, etc. But it implies that those employed at the management level and the millions who own their own small business do not work.

One of every four Americans owns corporate stock and benefits from the companies' profits, either directly or through an equity mutual fund. Millions more own stock through employer pension plans (which collectively own about one fourth of all corporate equity). Still others benefit as customers of insurance companies which invest in American businesses. In total, 70 percent of all equity (ownership) in American corporations is held by the general public, which is paid dividends based on profits. The value of the investors' shares rises as a result of the profits created by all the employees from the maintenance crew to the CEO.

How Capitalism Works

Profits, corporate and private, are the only sources of capital. Capital is the only source of more and better equipment to enable workers to be more productive, thus increasing their real wages and their standard of living. These are the root causes of the phenomenal growth of our gross national product over the past 150 years. This is the *why* and the *how* of our ability to increase the size of our economic pie by means of a system that functions for the benefit of all who are willing and able to work. Government now double-taxes corporate profits as well as the interest and dividends earned on private savings—hardly the best way to encourage the creation of capital.

No job done by hand can be done any faster today than it was over two hundred years ago. It is not possible for a man to earn more than a few dollars an hour for moving earth with a shovel, but give him a three-cubic-meter Caterpillar tractor and he can earn twenty-five dollars an hour or more. That is a prime example of industry's effect on our standard of living.

The investors who took the risk and provided the capital made it possible for a traveler to leave home in New York City and arrive in San Francisco 4½ hours later. He can do that because he has been given the benefit of some $10 billion in capital created from corporate profits and private savings and invested in the factories that produced the taxicabs he took to and from the airports; in the construction companies that built the superhighways over which he traveled and the extensive airport facilities he used; and in the company that designed and built the 747 jumbo jet that flew him across the continent. Only two hundred years ago it took more than two hundred dangerous and uncomfortable days to make that same trip with a capital investment of perhaps $200 (for a Conestoga wagon, horses, and other equipment).

Whether it be goods or services, the computer, the numerically controlled machining center, the tractor, the cellular telephone, or a thousand other miracles—their source is men and women who were free to pursue their dreams.

This is, however, a profit *and loss* system. Some succeed, but others fail and have to try again. Exactly what does the typical entrepreneur do, whether he is starting an enterprise with two employees or with two hundred?

1. He provides the capital required, borrowing or selling shares, if necessary.
2. He hires new employees.
3. He brings in raw materials from wherever necessary.
4. He produces a salable product.
5. He advertises and sells the product.
6. He pays the operating expenses, including wages.
7. He takes all the risks.

And having done all that, he then, according to the Department of Commerce, pays three times more in taxes than he pays himself, pays taxes again on whatever he *has* paid himself, and pays his employees roughly 19 times what he pays himself.

Even businesses themselves—whether large or small—are unaware of their tremendous contributions to their country. These are creative and daring people who work hard at all levels from the board room to the shop floor; who provide jobs, goods, services, and taxes; and who voluntarily support foundations, churches, hospitals, libraries, colleges, universities, and countless charities.

By any reasonable rationale, American businessmen should be considered public servants and benefactors; portrayed on the covers of *Time* and *Newsweek;* celebrated on CBS, NBC, and ABC; and held in high esteem by their government and their fellow citizens.

Unfortunately, such is not the case. Most businessmen are either unwilling or unable to challenge the vacuous and uninformed academics and demagogues who attack the business community and the free economic system of willing exchange. Indeed, businessmen themselves, claiming true faith in free enterprise, too often scramble to Washington, D.C., seeking legislation that will give them some theoretical edge. In doing so, they sow the seeds of their own destruction. Americans consume more because they produce more, but the interventionist mentality has little interest in how goods are produced; it is concerned only with how they are distributed. To suggest that the free market functions contrary to the interests of the poor is to reveal one's ignorance. No other system has done so much to wipe out poverty. A free market is not like a poker game where one man's stack of chips must go down for another's to go up. In a free economy, all the stacks can grow.

Nobel Laureate Friedrich A. von Hayek has probably expressed this truth as well as anyone else:

> There is one supreme myth which more than any other has served to discredit the economic system to which we owe our present day civilization. It is the legend of the deterioration of the position of the working classes in consequence of the rise of "Capitalism" or the "Industrial System."
>
> The wide-spread emotional aversion to "Capitalism" is closely connected with this belief that the undeniable growth of wealth which the competitive order had produced was purchased at the price of depressing the standard of life of the weakest elements of society. A more careful examination of the facts has, however, led to a thorough refutation of this belief.
>
> The freedom of economic activity which in England has proved so favorable to the rapid growth of wealth was probably in the first instance an almost accidental by-product of the limitations which the revolution of the 17th century had placed on the powers of government; and only after its beneficial effects had come to be widely noticed did the economists later undertake the connection and to argue for the removal of the remaining barriers to commercial freedom. We use the term Capitalism here because it is the most familiar name, but only with great reluctance, since with its modern connotations it is itself largely the creation of that socialistic interpretation of economic history with

which we are concerned. The term is especially misleading when, as is often the case, it is connected with the idea of the rise of the propertyless proletariat, which by some devious process has been deprived of their rightful ownership of the tools of their work.[5]

When Americans invested their earnings in new instruments of production to be operated by others who, without their help, would have had difficulty surviving, they put in place the springboard for America's economic miracle.

The increases in personal well-being and personal wealth raised aspirations as rapidly as they raised the standard of living, and the coming middle class began to emerge. Less than 3 percent of the population could be considered relatively well-to-do, even by the primitive standards of the day. The rest of the population was engaged in agriculture, attempting to solve the planet's most persistent problem—starvation. Today, less than 3 percent of the population is directly involved in agriculture, leaving the remaining 97 percent to fill all other areas of growth.

During this period the labor-displacement myth emerged, the theory that the introduction of machinery would reduce the demand for labor. It seemed to be a logical assumption, but history and statistics clearly demonstrate that precisely the opposite occurred. In some cases, new products and new companies came into being faster than available workers could be found. In others, the huge increases in sales volume in response to lower prices moved workers from one section of a manufacturing plant to another—and still mandated additional hiring.

Union leadership often claims credit for the dramatic improvements in our standard of living, but the fact is that by 1911—long before the union movement became powerful— wages in the United States were the highest in the world. Every worker, union member or not, deserves credit for being an integral member of the team that made it possible, but the productive and quality-control capabilities of machine tools were the essential elements. (I have, however, no quarrel with any union in which membership is voluntary.)

The rags-to-riches history of our great nation was written (and is still being written) by all individuals who contribute by doing their jobs to the best of their ability at every level and paying taxes to the various levels of government to protect our blessings of individual liberty and opportunity and to ensure our safety both at home and abroad. Some will rise higher on the ladder of economic well-being than others because both God and nature have seen to it that there are no two alike. In a free and ordered society, it is the responsibility of our elected officials to keep open the paths of opportunity. That is what we hire them to do, and we pay them well to do it. When, however, they attempt to ensure the outcomes of our individual efforts, they jeopardize our safety and our opportunity, and they should be replaced—none too gently.

As is often the case in any relationship, the major problems between business and the American public arise from inadequate communication. If everyone who provided capital and contributed to production were being praised for doing so by teachers from kindergarten through high school, by academics at the college and university level, by the media, and by elected officials, our children would begin to learn how a free society functions. After all, every government outlay or program is financed by *you.* If every recipient of funds dispensed through government agencies were told, "The funds for this program are, of course, being provided by your neighbors," credit would be given where credit is due.

Capitalism will not fail for lack of performance, but it may fail because the general public has been poorly educated and does not understand the source of its well-being.

Awhile back, I delivered some lectures at various colleges, universities, and high schools, and I developed a little game that generated surprising responses from the audience. (The idea for the game is gratefully credited to the late Leonard Read.) Try it with your children:

Let's pretend that it is 1871. We have come together to select one of five major tasks to accomplish. Our choices are:

1. To design and build a network of superhighways capable of handling whatever transportation requirements we expect to face 125 years from now in 1996.
2. To create a postal system equipped to cope with whatever the public might need in 1996.
3. To invent, manufacture, and market a box on which, with the turn of a knob, people can watch an event take place anywhere on earth—in color.
4. To invent a conveyance that will carry 350 people from coast to coast in less than five hours.
5. To invent a machine that will transmit a message around the earth in less than two minutes.

The young people will quickly agree that it would be silly to select an impossible project. Well, color television is obviously impossible. In 1871, you don't even have radio. The jumbo jet is also impossible, because you haven't even dreamt of the automobile in 1871. As for transmitting a message around the earth in two minutes or less—forget it. You just began stringing telegraph wires about 18 years ago, in 1853. Your version of instant communication consists of yelling across an open field, beating a drum, or sending a smoke signal.

The first two choices, however, are within the realm of possibility. The Romans built roads, so there might be a way to accomplish that. As far as a postal delivery system, we might be able to breed enough ponies to establish a really spectacular Pony Express.

The game makes the players realize that free men, working competitively and cooperatively, accomplished the impossible and worked the three "miracles" (and there were hundreds more). The two "possible" tasks were assigned to the federal government. The results? Many superhighways close to major cities resemble parking lots, and today you can ship four quarts of oil from the Persian Gulf to New York City for less than it costs you to send a letter across the street via the U.S. Post Office. Government does *not* excel at progress or problem solving.

It is time we start being proud of our accomplishments. Paradoxically, the most virulent critics of our way of life are usually quite well-to-do. Perhaps they suffer from guilt, but we cannot solve our problems by sleeping on a bed of nails. People who work productively are entitled to enjoy their rewards. Why should anyone feel guilty because the United States has achieved most of what the rest of the world strives for?

Those afflicted with martyrdom syndrome will say, "Isn't it awful that the United States with only 5 percent of the world's population consumes almost 30 percent of its energy?"

My response? "Isn't it incredible that the United States, with only a twentieth of the world's population, not only produces almost a third of the world's goods and services, but has become the industrial and agricultural breadbasket of the world? And aren't the people of the United States generous to have given more to the hungry and needy abroad than have all other nations put together?"

The constitutional purpose of government is to create an environment that leaves men and women free to utilize their creative energy by protecting them from fraud, coercion, and force. It was never the government's job to cripple our greatest asset—enterprise.

Notes

1. Karl Zinsmeister, "Payday Mayday," *American Enterprise* (Sept./Oct. 1995).
2. Henry Grady Weaver, *The Mainspring of Human Progress* (Irvington-on-Hudson, N.Y.: Foundation for Economic Education, 1953).
3. John M. Hood, *The Heroic Enterprise: Business and the Common Good* (New York: The Free Press, 1996).
4. Ibid.
5. Friedrich von Hayek, *Economic Myths of Early Capitalism* (Wilmington, Del.: Intercollegiate Studies Institute, 1960).

CHAPTER TEN

What Else We Know That Isn't So

The solution to America's problems does not lie primarily with political parties or in political action (although it eventually reverberates in these areas), nor does it lie in demonstrations or street marches. The solution to our problems is knowledge, the ability to recognize fallacious premises, and the ability to make decisions based on sound principles. The acquisition of such knowledge will not prevent us from disagreeing or from coming to opposing conclusions, but we will at least be playing the game with a full deck.

The solutions we seek lie in a general recognition of what is right and what is wrong, and in a general willingness to exert personal discipline to practice those virtues which typify a civil and orderly society.

As he traveled and studied what he referred to as "the miracle that is the United States," Alexis de Tocqueville observed:

> I think that in no country in the civilized world is less attention paid to philosophy than in the United States. The Americans have no philosophical school of their own; and they care but little for all the schools into which Europe is divided, the very names of which are scarcely known to them.

Nevertheless it is easy to perceive that almost all the inhabitants of the United States conduct their understanding in the same manner, and govern it by the same rules; that is to say, that without ever having taken the trouble to define the rules of a philosophical method, they are in possession of one, common to the whole people.[1]

That first paragraph is as valid today as it was in 1840, but the second paragraph is not. This absence of philosophy, this clouded understanding, *is* the problem. Work, faith, self-discipline, compassion, responsibility, friendship, courage, perseverance, honesty, and loyalty are the virtues that mark a civil society. And who will say that any nation would not be better if all its citizens practiced those virtues?

There is no easy route to such a goal. Our nation has undergone seismic changes, from a primarily agrarian society to an urban-industrial one, and it must contend with the problems of that new form. True, the adversity we face pales beside the difficulties faced by our forefathers, but the complexity of our world presents its own unique challenges. The principles governing our actions, however, have not changed.

Those principles are being flagrantly violated at the moment, but Newton's Law prevails in society as it does in physics: "For every action there will be an equal and opposite reaction." When this nation mobilizes to redress its wrongs, it will be another time of revolution.

It is understandable that a relatively large segment of our population accepts a myriad of labels (political and other), misused terms, economic myths, and just plain untruths. Given our educational shortcomings, and the mischief done by the media, it is no wonder that confusion reigns.

The Political Spectrum

The view of the political spectrum espoused by too many academics and most journalists (and passed on by them to our citizenry) places communism at the far left of the spectrum and fascism at the far right. A moderate, therefore, stands somewhere in the middle. No other paradigm could be less accurate.

Both communism and fascism foster regimented societies. Both adhere to socialistic principles—i.e., state ownership or control of the means of production and consumption. Both control the freedoms of their citizens. If these -*isms* are seen as opposite ends of the political spectrum, it becomes almost impossible sensibly to evaluate the state of individual liberty.

A proper model would place anarchy—a system of license and chaotic disorder—at one end of the spectrum. At the opposite end lie both communism and fascism. (A well-known political humorist once remarked: "A socialist will vehemently deny that he has any attachment to communism, but will find it impossible to explain *why* he doesn't.")

To diagram this nation's political spectrum, place Regimentation (i.e., Communism, Fascism, Socialism, Marxism) at the far left and Individual Liberty (i.e., Constitutional Republicanism, followers of John Adams et al.) at the far right.

REGIMENTATION					INDIVIDUAL LIBERTY
Communism	ALLEGED			ALLEGED	Constitutional
Fascism	PUBLIC			PUBLIC	Republic
Karl Marx	ATTITUDE			ATTITUDE	John Adams
	"A"	CENTERLINE		"B"	
	┊			┊	
D	┊	R	D	┊	R
	┊			┊	

The Center Line is just that. The two dotted lines (Alleged Public Attitudes A and B) represent the political parties' view of the attitude of the American public at any time. Their perception, however, is not necessarily accurate.

Public Attitude A represents the perception that, over the past forty years or so, the voting public has slipped to the left of center. Both parties, eager to position themselves in what they believed to be the politically popular spot, snuggled up on either side of the dotted line. The consequences? Candidates and legislation of a center-left posture—good or bad news, depending on your political persuasion.

During the 1994 congressional campaigns, for the first time in four decades, the Republican party placed itself in position B, leaving the Democratic party in position A The consequences? Both parties have shifted to the right, and the debate has shifted with them.

How does this interpretation affect the labels *liberal* and *conservative?* In Europe, those who believed in minimal government and maximum individual freedom were referred to as liberals. Logically so, because every nation on that continent lived under some form of royalty, and the citizens submitted to royal control. In the United States, those who believe in limited government are generally referred to as conservatives (or in media parlance, "right wing" conservatives), and those who believe in a large centralized government with considerable control over the citizenry are referred to as liberals. This mixture of definitions can lead to confusion—an anticommunist in Cincinnati was a conservative, but an anticommunist in Leningrad was a liberal. And it can lend itself to deliberate obfuscation—the media are fond of the term "right-wing extremist," but have apparently never encountered a "left-wing extremist."

Capitalism, the Rich, and the Poor

The conventional wisdom has been that capitalism favors the rich and socialism favors the poor. Earlier, however, we discussed the fact that the tools provided by capital make it possible for a worker to multiply his productivity and thus his wages. Higher productivity allows lower pricing, which increases the value of the worker's wages. Lower pricing also creates more demand. Increased demand creates more high-wage jobs. American history proves this. When our nation was founded, the approximate demographic breakdown was about 3 percent rich to 97 percent poor. Capitalism created the middle class and raised the percentage of well-to-do to an unimagined level, and it did so in an astonishingly short span of time.

There is also a prevalent notion that wealth is limited and, therefore, should be divided as evenly as possible. Throughout the world and throughout history, nations have attempted to redistribute the existing economic pie with little or no success. All economic command systems are based on the assumption that the amount of wealth is fixed, so their preoccupation has been with how goods are distributed, not with how they are produced. The genius of the American idea has been simply to bake bigger and bigger pies so that an ever-increasing segment of the population can prosper.

There is also considerable misunderstanding of inflation. To say that inflation causes prices to rise is like saying that floods cause torrential rains. Over the last thirty years government has spent approximately $5 trillion more than it has received in taxes. To pay its bills, it ran the printing presses overtime to create the necessary funds. Suppose you are playing Monopoly in your living room. You are running low on money, so you excuse yourself, go to the closet, and remove all the play money from a second Monopoly game. When you bring it back to the living room and introduce it into your game, what happens? You don't have any additional hotels or additional houses, no additional Park Places or Marvin Gardens, but you have double the money supply. The results? All prices double. That is classical inflation, and it is the primary cause of high prices.

However, there are other causes as well. Large wage settlements with unions, increased Social Security requirements, and the normal effects of supply and demand. The market logically decrees that things in short supply cost more, and things in oversupply cost less, so normal adjustments will even things out. Inflation is the primary culprit, but it is an effect of government overspending.

The Rich Get Richer

Doesn't everyone "know" that the rich do not pay their fair share of taxes? That is treated as a given in most debates about taxes, yet verified data released by the Tax Foundation reveals:

1. The top 1 percent of U.S. income earners paid 30.2 percent of individual income taxes in 1995. (Latest figures available.)
2. The top 5 percent paid 48.8 percent of all individual income taxes in 1995.
3. The top 10 percent of earners (the "rich" who make over $66,000) paid 60.5 percent of all income taxes in 1995.
4. The bottom 50 percent paid 4.8 percent of all income taxes in 1995.[2]

Who is not paying his or her fair share? When the government talks about raising taxes on the rich, the middle class should hold onto its wallet.

The National Debt

We are sometimes assured that we don't have to worry about the national debt because we owe it to ourselves. That debt is now over $5 trillion. The annual interest alone is galloping toward $350 billion. It is the single largest expense in our federal budget, surpassing defense spending in 1994 and Social Security in 1996. The federal debt is largely owed to the Federal Reserve banks, the International Monetary Fund, and private citizens who hold federal bonds and notes. Those U.S. Treasury bonds and notes establish the credit of the United States of America, and the interest *must* be paid. So we don't really "owe it to ourselves."

So can we agree that the only way to begin balancing the budget is to cut expenditures and raise taxes? The first part of that statement is absolutely correct. Profligate spending and waste are the keys to the problem. However, it is a fact that every time taxes are raised, the income received by the federal government drops. Whenever taxes are reduced (as during the Kennedy administration in 1962 and the Reagan administration in 1981), tax receipts increase. Why? Because taxpayers may be ill-informed, but they are not stupid. They react to tax hikes by reducing taxable income during high-tax cycles and increasing taxable income during low-tax cycles. In addition, tax reductions create incentives for entrepreneurial activity and the economy responds accordingly. High taxes always slow down the economy, and a strong economy is the source of government income.

The Reagan Years

Reporting on the Reagan presidency is a classic example of misrepresentation. Most of Reagan's detractors are fully aware of the facts, but choose to ignore them, so this is a response to the charges of economic malfeasance directed against the man and his administration:

Accusation: Under the Reagan administration, the rich got richer and poor got poorer.

Fact: Between 1980 and 1989, real after-tax income per person rose by 15.5 percent, and real median income of families, before taxes, went up 12.5 percent. Federal Reserve data shows that families with incomes between $10,000 and $50,000 a year experienced a higher percentage of growth in net worth than those in the top one-fifth income group.

Accusation: Under the Reagan administration the rich didn't pay their fair share of taxes.

Fact: Between 1980 and 1989, the top 1 percent not only paid more than 25 percent of all federal income taxes in 1990, but experienced a 40 percent increase over 1980. The bottom 60 percent paid only 11 percent of all income taxes in 1990, but paid 20 percent less in taxes than in 1980.

Accusation: Under the Reagan administration the safety net for the poor was destroyed.

Fact: Between 1980 and 1989, the total population below the poverty line decreased by 2.8 million people. Federal spending on the poor for income, food, health care, housing, education, training, and social services increased from $140 billion to $180 billion.

Accusation: Under the Reagan administration too much money was wasted on defense.

Fact: During the Kennedy administration, 48 percent of the federal budget was spent on defense. When Reagan took office, defense under President Carter had dropped to 21 percent of the federal budget. Reagan took it up to 31 percent during his eight years in office—and in the process contributed mightily to the demise of communism.

Accusation: Under the Reagan administration our deficits more than doubled.

Fact: When the tax cuts were put in place in 1983, revenues almost doubled, as they always do following a tax cut. It is true that the federal deficit skyrocketed, but it was the opposition Congress—not Reagan—that set off the exploding entitlement spending and created those deficits. Every budget Reagan sent to Congress was pronounced "dead on arrival."

As a consequence of Reagan's stewardship the United States experienced almost ninety-six months of continuous economic growth, the longest in peacetime history.

Do you remember the 21 percent interest rates? The 14 percent inflation rate? The massive unemployment that greeted Reagan when he took office? These problems were corrected almost overnight, and more new jobs were created than at any time since the end of World War II.

Words matter. If people are inundated with constant distortions, innuendoes, and misrepresentations that lead them to incorrect conclusions, the effect can be devastating.

Truth is relatively simple. It doesn't take kindly to spin doctors who deliberately manipulate our responses. Truth requires fewer words: the Lord's Prayer consists of only 56 words, the Ten Commandments of 392 words, and the Bill of Rights of 463. The Department of Agriculture's Federal Directive on Cabbage is 26,911 words long. What more can I say?

Notes

1. Tocqueville, *Democracy in America* (New York: Oxford University Press, 1952).
2. Tax Foundation, "IRS Report," *Human Events* (November 1997).

CHAPTER ELEVEN

The Lessons of History

The history of mankind teaches the immutable lesson that when men surrender control of their destinies to government in exchange for "social progress," they doom themselves and their posterity to personal regimentation and economic mediocrity. There has been no exception to this lesson, yet we seem determined to repeat that mistake.

As Paul Harvey reminds us, "You can't make the small man tall by cutting the legs off the giant." This misapprehension recalls the Greek legend of the giant Procrustes, who was convinced that he was the ideal size for a man. Consequently, he placed his captives in his own iron bed. Anyone too short to fit this bed was stretched to fit, and anyone too tall had his legs lopped off.

The fundamental question is, Do we wish to be responsible for our own futures? If the answer is no, then we are right to give up our freedom of choice and let the government determine our futures.

Responsibility and Control

Any individual has authority over whatever he takes responsibility for. If he abandons responsibility, government will gladly step in and assume authority over what would have been his areas of decision.

Freedom is the opportunity to make decisions, to choose among possible alternatives. Character is the ability to make morally correct decisions. As freedom diminishes, so may character. Government cannot make people good or happy or prosperous. Historically, after a a generation or two of government-managed society, the managed economy collapses and the resiliency and self-reliance of the citizenry are eroded. In 1922, for example, when Italy's experiment in collectivism failed, the people did not turn to a strong leader who would urge them to roll up their sleeves and set to work to solve their problems. Instead, they chose Benito Mussolini, who offered to solve their problems for them. Germany's pattern in 1933 was very similar, and Adolf Hitler was its consequence.

Government always claims to exercise power in the best interests of the people, whether that government is in the hands of a benevolent despot or of a tyrant like Hitler or Stalin. Today, however, the would-be despot must be subtler. If Paul can persuade the government to tax Peter and give the money to him, he can fulfill his own desires with a clear conscience because his action is altogether legal. And it may well be that neither Peter nor Paul will immediately perceive the power the government has acquired over both of them.

To those who value their personal liberty above all else, the magnitude of our problems is obvious. Having carefully examined what the relationship between man and government *ought* to be, we can see how far we have drifted from that ideal.

Perhaps, without realizing it, we have accepted the idea of freedom as a gift of the state in place of freedom as an inherent right. No matter what idealistic overtones color this error, it is still an error—and a deadly one. Would you trust a man who told you that he was going to commit an immoral act now so that he could be totally good later on? Probably not. The means condition the ends, and an evil act committed to achieve an alleged good will only contaminate the good. The late Judge Learned Hand put it this way:

> What do we mean when we say that first of all we seek liberty? I often wonder whether we do not rest our hopes too much upon constitutions, upon laws, and upon courts. These are false hopes; believe me these are false hopes. Liberty lies in the hearts of men and women; when it dies there, no constitution, no law, no court can save it.

Before we abdicate our responsibility and turn it over to government, we would do well to consider Milton Friedman's admonition (from *Capitalism and Freedom,* written over twenty years ago when our government was less than one fifth its current size):

> The power to do good is also the power to do harm; those who control the power today may not tomorrow; and, more important, what one man regards as good, another may regard as harm. The great tragedy of the drive to centralization, as of the drive to extend the scope of government in general, is that it is mostly led by men of good will who will be the first to rue its consequences.
>
> ... The greater part of the new ventures undertaken by government in the past few decades have failed to achieve their objectives. The United States has continued to progress; its citizens have become better fed, better clothed, better housed, and better transported; class and social distinctions have narrowed; minority groups have become less disadvantaged; popular culture has advanced by leaps and bounds. All this has been the product of the initiative and drive of the individuals cooperating through the free market. Government measures have hampered, not helped, this development. We have been able to afford and surmount these measures only because of the extraordinary fecundity of the market. The invisible hand has been more potent for progress than the visible hand for retrogressions.[1]

In short, we have progressed *in spite* of the growth of government power and intervention, not *because* of it.

In spite of the overwhelming weight of evidence, the paradox of our time is that an apparent majority of those in the political arena, in academia, and even in the business community continue to seek additional government intervention and control. It is only slightly less astonishing that the American people seem willing to go along.

As George Will put it, "Have America's voters chosen to be corrupted by the culture of pandemic government, the debasement of living larcenously off wealth created by others?"

The remark "When it comes to politics, Americans are not playing with a full deck—for the simple reason that they have not been dealt all of the cards" was originally spoken in jest—like many a true word. "Knowledge is power," and you can't find the algebraic *X* if you are missing half the equation. Deprivation of knowledge is certainly the heart of our dilemma, and it can destroy us. Edmund Burke said, "All that is necessary for evil to triumph is for good men to do nothing."

With that in mind, we will examine the workings of our political system.

Notes

1. Milton Friedman, *Capitalism and Freedom: Problems and Prospects* (Charlottesville: University of Virginia Press, 1975).

CHAPTER TWELVE

___

The Contentious World of Politics

My interest in government lies not in politics, but in the elements of a free and ordered society. It is true that our founders dealt in politics, but their primary concern was protecting individual freedom. History had made it clear that the greatest threat to liberty had always been the power of a centralized state, so they directed all our basic documents toward limiting that power. Most members of Congress and of the executive branch were answerable to constituents who would accept only minor incursions on their liberty. The politicians of the day understood the disastrous consequences of practicing political democracy, as opposed to the just and desirable results of maintaining a social democracy. They understood and feared majority rule and the risks it posed for a free society.

Where Have All the Statesmen Gone?

If he hopes to be a statesman, an elected representative listens to the views of his constituents, considers them with care, and makes his decisions based on sound judgment rather than on whether some or all of those constituents will approve. His responsibility is to ignore polls and other influences based on popularity. That is representative government.

To *represent* does not mean simply to ascertain what the public, the lobbyists, or the pressure groups want, and then to legislate accordingly. To do that is to place power and influence above correct principle and concern for the preservation of liberty.

What caused this massive shift from a constitutionally based democratic republic to an attempt at pure democracy? It was set in motion by the passage of the Sixteenth Amendment. The Income Tax Amendment profoundly altered the political environment. For the first time in our relatively short history, men in elective office were in a position to hand out other people's money in exchange for political support. The transition began slowly, then accelerated during the 1930s, and has virtually broken the sound barrier in recent years. Not all our legislators are practitioners of pure politics, but the ratio of statesmen to politicians has noticeably shrunk.

By way of a *caveat*, everything you have read here to this point is fact, or as close to fact as creditable research sources can provide. The notes and bibliography will allow you to verify that for yourself. This chapter, however, will contain both facts and opinions—though you will have little difficulty distinguishing one from the other.

Knowledge and Power

People acquire two distinct types of knowledge. Secondary knowledge is that which we employ in our jobs or professions, whatever they may be. It is the knowledge or know-how by which we earn our living; it is a tool of survival.

Primary knowledge is the stuff of purposes and values—the understanding of the relationship between man and his Creator; man and his fellow man, and man and his government. The product of this primary knowledge is what I prefer to call peace of mind (rather than "mental health"). It allows us to recognize our responsibility and/or our higher purpose.

In a free and ordered society, primary knowledge is essential for improving and enhancing one's life and for protecting one's individual freedom. In a regimented society, primary knowledge is unnecessary. Citizens have already surrendered most, if not all, of their individual liberties and are essentially wards of the state. Consequently, basic needs, at least theoretically, have been provided. People have no need to make decisions, to develop discipline, or to answer for their own actions. They have, in a very real sense, traded their birthright of liberty for a mess of pottage.

We are, as we have seen, deficient in primary knowledge relating to our heritage. Most members of the media were also deprived, but it is a journalist's responsibility to seek the truth and report it, not to dissemble, accept the conventional wisdom without question, and end up telling us *what we know that isn't so.*

It is our responsibility to question as well. We must not soak up television sound bites and the interpretations of news analysts as if they were gospel truths; we must apply a little common sense. We are right to be anxious about our future. The subconscious attitudes of the political establishment would turn us from free citizens back into mere colonists. And both political parties must share the blame. Like King George III and his Parliament, they have *"erected a multitude of New Offices, and sent hither swarms of Officers to harass our People, and eat out their substance."* They stand accused of *"imposing taxes on us without our Consent"* and of making *"Judges dependent on his Will alone, for the tenure of their offices and the amount and payment of their salaries."* The founders refused to stand for it.

What About Us?

Serious as our dilemma is, I can't help thinking of the words Oliver Hardy addressed to Stan Laurel: "Another fine mess you've gotten us in!" We should carve that in marble over the House and Senate chambers and on the west portico of the White House.

Politics as Usual

Our government preaches the benefits of free market capitalism to the rest of the world while legislating us into socialism. Politics deals with the issues of power, influence, and control, and while our founding fathers sought to keep these factors in the hands of the people, too many of today's politicians are bent on snatching them back.

If you read Niccolò Machiavelli's *The Prince* and *The Discourses,* you will find masterly lessons in the acquisition and maintenance of political control. The two fundamental principles of leadership, according to Machiavelli, are these:

1. Create a situation that places the vast majority of the population in a position of dependency on the centralized authority.
2. Divide the population into as many polarized segments as possible which, on the one hand, prevents them from uniting with any significant opposition to the centralized authority. In addition, by keeping the factions divided and hostile to one another, they perceive that each of them must rely on the centralized authority for protection from the other antagonists.[1]

Machiavelli was concerned with political control over Italy's principalities. By fostering warfare between them, a leader could make each one dependent on him for defense against the others. Divide and conquer.

The adjective *Machiavellian* is commonly used to denote "corrupt and devious." When he describes the behavior required to succeed as a leader, it is not difficult to see why:

1. Appear compassionate—but be ruthless; lie, cheat, and mislead, for power is the objective.
2. The end always justifies the means. He who has the gold makes the rules.
3. Deceit is the road to power.

4. Get religion out of politics.
5. Appearance is more important than reality.
6. Appear as a Christian—but show your enemies hell.
7. Appear virtuous—but inflict pain.[2]

To a modern reader, this description is appalling, yet Machiavelli's suggestions have been adapted over the years, and we see shadows of them even now. Conscious efforts are made to encourage warfare between races, between men and women, between gays and straights, between rich and poor. Inflammatory rhetoric is tolerated. Class envy is becoming the political weapon of choice. People who own a home, an automobile, and three television sets, and live at a level beyond their early expectations are told that they are being deprived because others own a larger home, have two automobiles, etc. It is an unforgivable exercise in manipulation.

In 1993, according to Bob Woodward, one of the president's chief political advisors suggested that the most important reason to pass a National Health Care Act was so that the government could acquire of 25 million additional dependents—not so Americans would get an improved health care system.[3]

Political labels are tossed around without regard for truth or logic. An "extremist" is anyone who disagrees with the media, anyone who wishes to return to constitutional principles and reduce the size and scope of the federal government.

I would be surprised if there were any politicians on either side of the aisle who do not wish to help the less fortunate. Yet when alternative ideas are put forth to replace the flagrantly failed policies of the last three decades, they are immediately labeled harsh, cruel, and unfeeling. They are precisely the opposite, but the media apply these appellations to anyone who disagrees with them. (Again, not all members of the electronic and print media are so careless, but the vast majority are.) The Christian Coalition was simply a group of Christians, until it began to take political positions. Now it is a group of "right-wing extremists."

Who are the extremists? Those who steer our nation away from constitutional principles? Or those who attempt to return us to a free and ordered society?

We are in this fix in large part because of what the late Leonard Read referred to as "The Exception Makers":

> "I am for free-enterprise, but I favor Federal Aid to Education."

> "I believe that every person has the right to the fruits of his own labor, but I favor progressive and graduated income taxes and compulsory Social Security."

> "I stand foursquare for private property, but we need subsidized navigation in order to obtain cheaper coal for our steam plant."

> "I subscribe to the principles of limited government, but it's all right for the State to prescribe and enforce minimum wages and maximum hours of work."

Washington, D.C., is a bee-hive of exception makers:

- "I believe in a balanced budget, but ... "
- "I believe in reducing the size of government, but ..."
- "I believe in lowering confiscatory taxes, but ..."

Government, by and large, talks free market, but walks socialism. The term *successful socialism* is a classic oxymoron. It doesn't exist, and it never has.

Politics Now

The U.S. Senate operates under a completely different set of rules from those of the House. The founders clearly intended that one of the Senate's functions would be to prevent the hasty passage of radical or impractical legislation.

Following Senate-House conferences in 1994, Congress passed the Balanced Budget Act, designed to end deficit spending by the year 2002, while providing tax cuts directed primarily to middle-class taxpayers and a capital gains tax designed to spur economic growth and thus provide employment opportunity; a welfare bill designed to turn the program toward work requirements and begin to eliminate the disastrous levels of poverty created by earlier government legislation; and Medicare/Medicaid legislation designed to slow down costs that have been rising at more than three times the rate of inflation and to allow senior citizens additional health-care choices. In every case, payments to recipients and spending levels would actually *increase* over the subsequent seven years, though at a much slower rate.

Not unexpectedly, the president vetoed all these bills, so they were put in the form of Continuing Resolutions in order to fund the government temporarily (following a brief shutdown), and the debate between Congress and the administration began anew.

There was a particularly unsavory aspect to the debate in the 104th Congress. Politics has always involved heated debates and even furious exchanges. During the mid-1800s disagreements led to an occasional duel. The atmosphere in this Congress, however, reached an unprecedented level of vitriol and mendacity—largely coming from one side of the aisle.

The 104th Congress worked night and day to produce carefully thought-out proposals embracing both fiscal sanity and compassion. The opposition offered no alternative legislation (although the president's budget creating $200 billion in deficits was voted down unanimously by both sides of the aisle).

Those who held onto power for forty years "went ballistic," calling the new legislation "extremist ... harsh ... cruel ... radical," and charging that "You're trying to starve children and the elderly" or "You're throwing people into the streets" or "You want dirty air and dirty water."

No alternatives were offered by liberal members of Congress or by the president, only attempts to frighten with complete untruths the most defenseless in our society. It's the exception makers again:

"I'm for a balanced budget, but . . ."
"I'm for Medicare reform, but . . ."
"I'm for everything, but I'm not willing to do what is necessary to achieve it."

Is balancing the budget when a five-trillion-dollar deficit hangs over our heads extreme?

Is saving Medicare from bankruptcy extreme?

Is overhauling a welfare system that has increased poverty for thirty years extreme?

Exhausted by the battles in the 104th Congress, in 1997 the 105th Congress passed, and the president signed, a largely cosmetic "Balanced Budget Act," putting off until another day facing these serious issues.

Truth is a rare commodity in the world of politics as it is currently practiced. When truth reemerges, statesmanship will come with it.

Notes

1. Niccolò Machiavelli, *The Prince* and *The Discourses* (New York: Modern Library, 1950).
2. Ibid.
3. Robert Woodward, *The Agenda* (New York: Simon & Schuster, 1993).

CHAPTER THIRTEEN

Assumptions, Principles, and Observations

A long-standing recommendation to authors and lecturers suggests the following formula:

1. First you tell them what you're going to tell them.
2. Then you tell them.
3. Then you tell them what you told them.

The fundamental assumption of this tract is that almost everyone would prefer to live in a nation where:

1. Individual freedom is maximized.
2. Opportunity is maximized.
3. Personal safety is maximized.
4. Prosperity is the rule rather than the exception.

The alternatives certainly don't appeal to me:

1. Individual freedom is minimized.
2. Opportunity is minimized.
3. Personal safety is threatened.
4. Prosperity is the exception rather than the rule.

Since people from all over the world continue to "vote with their feet" by flocking to our shores (and there is no opposite phenomenon, whereby people leave the United States in droves to seek a better life elsewhere), I further assume that my preferences are widely shared.

Not everyone who reads this book, of course, will agree with what appear to me to be obvious conclusions, but that in a way is my point: Everyone has the freedom and the right to pick and choose, to agree or disagree. I simply want to give readers the other half of the equation, the full deck, the information on which they can base their choices.

Another assumption made here is that human nature adheres to its self-interest, and that that is a good thing so long as it does not produce behavior that is detrimental to one's fellow citizens. This country had such an arrangement firmly in place, a system wherein every individual's success benefited others directly or indirectly, through willing exchange and protection from fraud, coercion, and force. We are losing that system, letting it slip away, but we can regain it.

More than three decades of legislation and court decisions have created conditions far worse than those they were designed to correct. Our problems are extremely serious and the current environment is having a devastating effect on our fundamental values and those of our children. That is why I feel a sense of urgency. Clearly, however, some of these problems will require long-term solutions. Indeed, some will take decades to correct. The education of today's citizens and of the generations to follow is probably the single most important element in our recovery, and it will certainly take many years to remedy. Other problems can be solved more quickly, but we must be wary of impulsive and politically popular solutions: "Legislate in haste, repent at leisure."

Consider the minimum wage laws and the Family Leave Act. Both sound good, but their consequences have run counter to their intent. Both create unemployment and raise the price of goods and services. Look in Appendix B, and see if you can find any provision that allows the federal government to meddle with wages or prices. Those are within the province of the free market, and consumers are perfectly capable of such determinations.

As quoted earlier, Thomas Jefferson warned, "If a nation, in a state of civilization, expects to be ignorant and free, it expects what never was and never will be." And John Adams (see Chapter 5) declared, "Our Constitution was made for a moral and religious people. It is wholly inadequate to the government of any other."

To improve education K through 12, we must remove the federal government and return responsibility for, and control of, our schools to the states and the local communities. We must introduce the element of competition into education through the exercise of free choice. We must allow voluntary prayer (as we do in the Congress itself) and let today's dedicated teachers know that they—and we—have been deprived of important information. (Expect a head-on collision with the leadership of the National Education Association.) But the solutions to both the education crisis and the weakening of our "moral and religious" society lie primarily within the home and family.

The foundation of any sustained effort to end the fiscal insanity that has plagued us since 1969 must be policies that will bring about real, sustained, robust economic growth. This can be accomplished without inflation if the incentives are properly directed.

To begin with, the federal budget must be balanced and kept in balance, and the only way to accomplish that is to increase revenues and reduce government expenditures. To increase revenues, we must cut taxes. The Cato Institute reports that, after the Reagan tax cuts, revenues rose 24 percent over the following seven years. If federal revenues had grown in the 1990s at the pace they did after the Reagan tax cuts, 1996 revenues would be $50 billion greater and the deficit would be one third smaller. As for expenditure reductions, there are more targets than you can count.

With the exception of the 104th Congress, the federal legislative branch has not balanced the budget since 1969.

Congress has proven itself incapable of fiscal control. I, therefore, suggest a Constitutional Amendment setting spending limits for any year at a fixed percentage of the previous year's Gross Domestic Product (a number difficult to distort). This means that, after the debate to determine the permanently set percentage (suppose it is set at 20 percent), Congress would know that total expenditures for the next fiscal year would be X dollars. They would still debate to determine how those dollars would be spent, but since they had proven themselves incapable of setting their own limits, their allowance of your money would be pre-set. (Don't hold your breath till this idea is enacted into law.)

For readers who wonder what they as individuals can do, my first recommendation is that they watch pending legislation. True, federal legislation is often so complex that it's hard to decide where you stand. In such cases, apply the method an old friend of mine has proposed (I call it Campaigne's Law): If you don't feel that you have adequate information about a proposition, simply find out who's for it, and who's against it. More often than not, you'll arrive at your position with ease.

I also recommend that you support any proposition that:

1. Reduces the size of the federal establishment.
2. Moves power away from Washington, D.C., and returns it to the states.
3. Reduces taxes.
4. Reduces or eliminates regulations.
5. Privatizes any function now being handled by the bureaucracy.
6. Reduces the number of federal employees.
7. Eliminates the Departments of Commerce, Education, Housing and Urban Development, Labor, Energy, and Environmental Protection Agency.
8. Eliminates the Small Business Administration and/or the Federal Communications Commission.
9. Privatizes the Post Office.

10. Eliminates at least 80 percent of the 1,250-plus Advisory Boards, Commissions, Committees,and Panels.

There is a basic law of the human psyche, as immutable as the law of gravity: Becoming first requires overcoming. If we were starting over and seeking commonsense remedies for our problems, the task would be relatively easy. Unfortunately, we must address our problems from where we are now, which is much more difficult and far more contentious, and proceeds at a much slower rate than many of us would desire. Nevertheless, the benefits of redressing the damage done by decades of serious misdirection will still yield, at the very least, these benefits:

1. A great increase in economic growth and available jobs.
2. A higher standard of living.
3. Much improved education for our children.
4. Safety on our streets.
5. Lower taxes.
6. Greater job security.

In at least one sense, the difference between liberals and conservatives today can be summed up this way:

1. Today's Conservative believes that the mainspring of a free society is the opportunity for every individual to strive for "upward inequality."
2. Today's Liberal believes that the purpose of a free society is to create "artificial equality."

Our primary concern should be self-improvement in the sense of advancing our understanding and our ability to articulate the principles and values to which we adhere. This is the single most important long-range contribution we can make toward the restoration of our economic and personal liberty.

The case for the free market or willing-exchange economy rests primarily on its economic efficiency and its miraculous ability to advance man's material well-being. Still, I'm inclined to agree with Dr. Benjamin Rogge that another factor is even more important:

> My central thesis is that the most important part of the case for economic freedom is not its vaunted efficiency as a system for organized resources, not its tremendous success in promoting economic growth, but rather its consistency with certain fundamental moral principles of life itself.
>
> I say, "the most important part of the case" for two reasons. First, the significance I attach to those moral principles would lead me to prefer the free enterprise system even if it were demonstrably *less* efficient than alternative systems, even if it were to produce a *slower* rate of growth than systems of central direction and control. Second, the great mass of the people of any country is never going to really understand the purely economic workings of any economic system, be it free enterprise or socialism. Hence, most people are going to judge an economic system by its consistency with their moral principles rather than by its purely scientific operating characteristics. If economic freedom survives in the years ahead, it will be only because the majority of the people accept its basic morality.[1]

Let me pose this question: *If* we had the economic and philosophical knowledge; *if* we had the time, the staff, and the ability to write, articulate, and debate the issues; *if* we had *all* these things and more, how would we use them to meet this challenge successfully?

1. We would become involved in the formulation of public opinion by participating in television and radio talk shows and public opinion forums of all types, debating issues and philosophies with academics, politicians, etc. We would write regular editorial replies and letters promoting the free market philosophy to the editors of major journals and newspapers.
2. We would create and work with research foundations

to provide the information necessary to enlighten elected representatives.

3. We would monitor state and federal legislation at all stages, from the committee to the floor, and blitz our representatives with telephone calls and letters on important issues.

4. We would propose, sponsor, and write tax-limitation bills, constitutional amendments requiring budget balancing, and legislation involving other pertinent issues.

5. We would create and support colleges and universities dedicated to advancing the free market philosophy, and we would participate in adult education foundations by finding available lecturers and writers who can take the case to the public.

6. We would lobby actively at federal and state levels not for our own businesses or industries, but rather for whatever encourages a free market environment. We would defend the producing segments of our nation when they are under attack and expect them to do the same when our industry is besieged.

7. We would monitor and create semi-annual voting records of federal and state legislators, and publicize the results. Such efforts help to expose public servants who campaign in one posture and, once elected, support opposing legislation.

8. We would locate, educate, and promote at all levels political candidates who support the free market position.

We need to become skilled at rebutting irresponsible journalism. Teachers, politicians, columnists, television news analysts, and playwrights can disseminate erroneous theory by generating emotional appeals for their causes. The businessman, large or small, goes out of business if he operates on erroneous theory.

At present we are simply not in a position to accomplish

most of these tasks. Why? Because most of these activities are outside our areas of expertise. What *do* we do now in such areas (e.g., law, computer technology, public relations, taxes, advertising, etc.)? We recognize our limitations and contract or hire people with the necessary knowledge and experience.

There are many organizations and individuals involved in such work, but four in particular merit special attention:

The Heritage Foundation
Edwin J. Feulner, Jr., President
214 Massachusetts Avenue, N.E.
Washington, D.C. 20002
Telephone: (202) 546-4400

Heritage has had unparalleled success as the largest policy research foundation dedicated to the principles of free enterprise, individual freedom, and a strong national security policy. It provides erudite analysis and position papers keyed to pending legislation. Ask for the book *Rolling Back Government,* as fine a piece of research on the subject as I have ever encountered. Support them monetarily as much as possible.

Intercollegiate Studies Institute
T. Kenneth Cribb, President
3901 Centerville Road
Wilmington, Del. 19807
Telephone: (302) 652-4600

For over forty-six years ISI has been active on college campuses. Its success in undoing almost ninety years of contrary efforts by the Intercollegiate Socialist Society has been phenomenal. Its seminars, lectures, publications, and campus magazine have a significant impact throughout the academic community. ISI deserves strong financial support.

The Cato Institute
1000 Massachusetts Avenue, N.W.
Washington, D. C. 20001
Telephone: (202) 842-0200

Cato is one of the most rapidly growing think tanks in D.C. Its research, position papers, and testimonies before congressional committees are highly effective. Ask for the *Handbook for Congress,* a splendid piece of work. Support Cato financially if you possibly can.

Educational Research Institute
National Journalism Center
M. Stanton Evans, President
800 Maryland Avenue
Washington, D.C. 20002
Telephone: (202) 546-1710

The National Journalism Center provides a successful antidote to the serious problem of media bias by graduating highly competent journalists with a predilection toward the principles of a free and ordered society. Give it financial support to the best of your ability, because it is working to counteract *what we know that isn't so.*

It has not been my purpose here to change anyone's mind. My purpose is to inform and perhaps to engender appreciation of the brilliant statesmen who gave us our freedom and the foundation for our opportunities and our standard of living. My purpose is also to raise the question, "How can we make intelligent decisions about political matters if we have seen only one side of the equation?"

No future historian will ever be able to say that the ideas of individual liberty once practiced in the United States of America were a failure. It might be said, however, that we were not worthy of them.

The choice is still ours.

Notes
1. Benjamin A. Rogge, *The Case for Economic Freedom* (Irvington-on-Hudson, N.Y.: Foundation for Economic Education, 1963).

The Declaration of Independence
In Congress, July 4, 1776

The Unanimous Declaration of the Thirteen United States of America

When in the Course of human events, it becomes necessary for one people to dissolve the political bands which have connected them with another, and to assume among the Powers of the earth, the separate and equal station to which the Laws of Nature and of Nature's God entitle them, a decent respect to the opinions of mankind requires that they should declare the causes which impel them to the separation.

We hold these truths to be self-evident, that all men are created equal, that they are endowed by their Creator with certain unalienable Rights, that among these are Life, Liberty, and the pursuit of Happiness. That to secure these rights, Governments are instituted among Men, deriving their just powers from the consent of the governed. That whenever any Form of Government becomes destructive of these ends, it is the Right of the People to alter or to abolish it, and to institute new Government, laying its foundation on such principles and organizing its powers in such form, as to them shall seem most likely to effect their Safety and Happiness. Prudence, indeed, will dictate that Governments long established should not be changed for light and transient causes; and accordingly all experience hath shown, that mankind are more disposed to suffer, while evils are sufferable, than to right themselves by abolishing the forms to which they are accustomed. But when a long train of abuses and usurpations, pursuing invariably but same Object evinces a design to reduce them under absolute Despotism, it is their right, it is their duty, to throw off such Government, and to provide new Guards for their future security.

Such has been the patient sufferance of these Colonies; and such is now the necessity which constrains them to alter their former Systems of Government. The history of the present King of Great Britain is a history of repeated injuries and usurpations, all having in direct object the establishment of an absolute Tyranny over these States. To prove this, let Facts be submitted to a candid world.

He has refused his Assent to Laws, the most wholesome and necessary for the public good.

He has forbidden his Governors to pass Laws of immediate and pressing importance, unless suspended in their operation till his Assent should be obtained; and when so suspended, he has utterly neglected to attend to them.

He has refused to pass other Laws for the accommodation of large districts of people, unless those people would relinquish the right of Representation in the Legislature, a right inestimable to them and formidable to tyrants only.

He has called together legislative bodies at places unusual, uncomfortable, and distant from the depository of their Public Records, for the sole purpose of fatiguing them into compliance with his measures.

He has dissolved Representative Houses repeatedly, for opposing with manly firmness his invasions on the rights of the people.

He has refused for a long time, after such dissolutions, to cause others to be elected; whereby the Legislative Powers, incapable of Annihilation, have returned to the People at large for their exercise; the State remaining in the mean time exposed to all the dangers of invasion from without, and convulsions within.

He has endeavoured to prevent the population of these States; for that purpose obstructing the Laws for Naturalization of Foreigners; refusing to pass others to encourage their migration hither, and raising the conditions of new Appropriations of Lands.

He has obstructed the Administration of Justice, by refusing his Assent to Laws for establishing Judiciary Powers.

He has made Judges dependent on his Will alone, for the tenure of their offices, and the amount and payment of their salaries.

He has erected a multitude of New Offices, and sent hither swarms of Officers to harass our People, and eat out their substance.

He has kept among us, in times of peace, Standing Armies without the Consent of our legislatures.

He has affected to render the Military independent of and superior to the Civil Power.

He has combined with others to subject us to a Jurisdiction foreign to our constitution, and unacknowledged by our laws; giving his Assent to their Acts of pretended Legislation:

For quartering large bodies of armed troops among us:

For protecting them, by mock Trial, from Punishment for any Murders which they should commit on the Inhabitants of these States:

For cutting off our Trade with all parts of the world:

For imposing taxes on us without Consent:

For depriving us in many cases, of the benefits of Trial by Jury:

For transporting us beyond Seas to be tried for pretended offences:

For abolishing the free System of English Laws in a neighbouring

Province, establishing therein an Arbitrary government, and enlarging its boundaries so as to render it at once an example and fit instrument for introducing the same absolute rule into these Colonies:

For taking away our Charters, abolishing our most valuable Laws, and altering fundamentally the Forms of our Government:

For suspending our own Legislatures, and declaring themselves invested with Power to legislate for us in all cases whatsoever.

He has abdicated Government here, by declaring us out of his Protection and waging War against us.

He has plundered our seas, ravaged our Coasts, burnt our towns, and destroyed the lives of our people.

He is at this time transporting large Armies of foreign Mercenaries to complete the works of death, desolation and tyranny, already begun with circumstances of Cruelty and perfidy scarcely paralleled in the most barbarous ages, and totally unworthy the Head of a civilized nation.

He has constrained our fellow Citizens taken Captive on the high Seas to bear Arms against their Country, to become the executioners of their friends and Brethren, or to fall themselves by their Hands.

He has excited domestic insurrections amongst us, and has endeavoured to bring on the inhabitants of our frontiers, the merciless Indian Savages, whose known rule of warfare, is an undistinguished destruction of all ages, sexes and conditions.

In every stage of these oppressions We have Petitioned for Redress in the most humble terms: Our repeated Petitions have been answered only by repeated injury. A Prince, whose character is thus marked by every act which may define a Tyrant, is unfit to be the ruler of a free People.

Nor have We been wanting in attention to our British brethren. We have warned them from time to time of attempts by their legislature to extend an unwarrantable jurisdiction over us. We have reminded them of the circumstances of our emigration and settlement here. We have appealed to their native justice and magnanimity, and we have conjured them by the ties of our common kindred to disavow these usurpations, which would inevitably interrupt our connections and correspondence. They too have been deaf to the voice of justice and of consanguinity. We must, therefore, acquiesce in the necessity, which denounces our Separation, and hold them, as we hold the rest of mankind, Enemies in War, in Peace Friends.

We, therefore, Representatives of the United States of America, in General Congress, Assembled, appealing to the Supreme Judge of the world for the rectitude of our intentions, do, in the Name, and by the Authority of the good People of these Colonies, solemnly publish and declare, That these United Colonies are, and of Right out to be Free and Independent States; that they are Absolved from all Allegiance to the British Crown, and that all political connection between them and the State of Great Britain, is and ought to be totally dissolved; and that as Free and Independent States, they have full Power to levy War, conclude Peace, contract Alliances, establish Commerce, and to do all other Acts and Things which Independent States may of right do. And for the support of this Declaration, with a firm reliance on the Protection of divine Province, we mutually pledge to each other our Lives, our Fortunes and our sacred Honor.

Constitution of the United States

WE THE PEOPLE of the United States, in Order to form a more perfect Union, establish Justice, insure domestic Tranquillity, provide for the common defence, promote the general Welfare, and secure the Blessings of Liberty to ourselves and our Posterity, do ordain and establish this Constitution for the United States of America.

Article I

SECTION 1. All legislative Powers herein granted shall be vested in a Congress of the United States, which shall consist of a Senate and House of Representatives.

SECTION 2. The House of Representatives shall be composed of Members chosen every second Year by the People of the several States, and the Electors in each State shall have the Qualifications requisite for Electors of the most numerous Branch of the State Legislature.

No Person shall be a Representative who shall not have attained to the Age of twenty five Years, and been seven Years a Citizen of the United States, and who shall not, when elected, be an Inhabitant of that State in which he shall be chosen.

Representatives and direct Taxes shall be apportioned among the several States which may be included within this Union, according to their respective Numbers, which shall be determined by adding to the whole Number of free Persons, including those bound to Service for a Term of Years, and excluding Indians not taxed, three fifths of all other Persons. The actual Enumeration shall be made within three Years after the first Meeting of the Congress of the United States, and within every subsequent Term of ten Years, in such Manner as they shall by Law direct. The Number of Representatives shall not exceed one for every thirty Thousand, but each State shall have at Least one Representative; and until such enumeration shall be made, the State of New Hampshire shall be entitled to chuse three, Massachusetts eight, Rhode-Island and Providence Plantations one, Connecticut five, New-York six, New Jersey four, Pennsylvania eight, Delaware one, Maryland six, Virginia ten, North Carolina five, South Carolina five, and Georgia three.

When vacancies happen in the Representation from any State, the Executive Authority thereof shall issue Writs of Election to fill such Vacancies.

The House of Representatives shall chuse their Speaker and other Officers; and shall have the sole Power of Impeachment.

SECTION 3. The Senate of the United States shall be composed of two Senators from each State, chosen by the Legislature thereof, for six Years; and each Senator shall have one Vote.

Immediately after they shall be assembled in Consequence of the first Election, they shall be divided as equally as may be into three Classes. The seats of the Senators of the first Class shall be vacated at the Expiration of the second Year, of the second Class at the Expiration of the fourth year, and of the third Class at the Expiration of the sixth Year, so that one third may be chosen every second Year; and if Vacancies happen by Resignation, or otherwise, during the Recess of the Legislature of any State, the Executive thereof may make temporary Appointments until the next Meeting of the Legislature, which shall then fill such Vacancies.

No Person shall be a Senator who shall not have attained to the Age of thirty Years, and been nine Years a Citizen of the United States, and who shall not, when elected, be an Inhabitant of that State for which he shall be chosen.

The Vice President of the United States shall be President of the Senate, but shall have no Vote, unless they be equally divided.

The Senate shall chuse their other Officers, and also a President pro tempore, in the Absence of the Vice President, or when he shall exercise the Office of President of the United States.

The Senate shall have the sole Power to try all Impeachments. When sitting for that Purpose, they shall be on Oath or Affirmation. When the President of the United States is tried, the Chief Justice shall preside: And no Person shall be convicted without the Concurrence of two thirds of the Members present.

Judgment in Cases of Impeachment shall not extend further than to removal from Office, and disqualification to hold and enjoy any Office of honor, Trust or Profit under the United States: but the Party convicted shall nevertheless be liable and subject to Indictment, Trial, Judgment and Punishment, according to Law.

SECTION 4. The Times, Places and Manner of holding Elections for Senators and Representatives, shall be prescribed in each State by the Legislature thereof; but the Congress may at any time by Law make or alter such Regulations, except as to the Places of chusing Senators.

The Congress shall assemble at least once in every Year, and such Meeting shall be on the first Monday in December, unless they shall by Law appoint a different Day.

SECTION 5. Each House shall be the Judge of the Elections, Returns and Qualifications of its own Members, and a Majority of each shall constitute a Quorum to do Business; but a smaller Number may adjourn from day to day, and may be authorized to compel the Attendance of absent Members, in such Manner, and under such Penalties as each House may provide.

Each House may determine the Rules of its Proceedings, punish its Members for disorderly Behavior, and, with the Concurrence of two thirds, expel a Member.

Each House shall keep a Journal of its Proceedings, and from time to time publish the same, excepting such Parts as may in their Judgment require Secrecy; and the Yeas and Nays of the Members of either House on any question shall, at the Desire of one fifth of those Present, be entered on the Journal.

Neither House, during the Session of Congress, shall, without the Consent of the other, adjourn for more than three days, nor to any other Place than that in which the two Houses shall be sitting.

SECTION 6. The Senators and Representatives shall receive a Compensation for their Services, to be ascertained by Law, and paid out of the Treasury of the United States. They shall in all Cases, except Treason, Felony and Breach of the Peace, be privileged from Arrest during their Attendance at the Session of their respective Houses, and in going to and returning from the same; and for any Speech or Debate in either House, they shall not be questioned in any other Place.

No Senator or Representative shall, during the Time for which he was elected, be appointed to any civil Office under the Authority of the United States, which shall have been created, or the Emoluments whereof shall have been encreased during such time; and no Person holding any Office under the United States, shall be a Member of either House during his Continuance in Office.

SECTION 7. All Bills for raising Revenue shall originate in the House of Representatives; but the Senate may propose or concur with Amendments as on other Bills.

Every Bill which shall have passed the House of Representatives and the Senate, shall, before it become a Law, be presented to the President of the United States; If he approve he shall sign it, but if not he shall return it, with his Objections to that House in which it shall have originated, who shall enter the Objections at large on their Journal, and proceed to reconsider it. If after such Reconsideration two thirds of that House shall agree to pass the Bill, it shall be sent, together with the Objections, to the other House, by which it shall likewise be reconsidered, and if approved by two thirds of that House, it shall become a Law. But in all such Cases the Votes of both Houses shall be determined by Yeas and Nays, and the Names of the Persons voting for and against the Bill shall be entered on the Journal of each House respectively. If any Bill shall not be returned by the President within ten Days (Sundays excepted) after it shall have been presented to him, the Same shall be a Law, in like Manner as if he had signed it, unless the Congress by their Adjournment prevent its Return, in which Case it shall not be a law.

Every Order, Resolution, or Vote to which the Concurrence of the Senate and House of Representatives may be necessary (except on a question of Adjournment) shall be presented to the President of the United States; and before the Same shall take Effect, shall be approved by him, or being disapproved by him, shall be repassed by two thirds of the Senate and House of Representatives, according to the Rules and Limitations prescribed in the Case of a Bill.

SECTION 8. The Congress shall have Power To lay and collect Taxes, Duties, Imposts and Excises, to pay the Debts and provide for the common Defence and general Welfare of the United States; but all Duties, Imposts and Excises shall be uniform throughout the United States;

To borrow Money on the credit of the United States;

To regulate Commerce with foreign Nations, and among the several States, and with the Indian Tribes;

To establish an uniform Rule of Naturalization, and uniform Laws on the subject of Bankruptcies throughout the United States;

To coin Money, regulate the Value thereof, and of foreign Coin, and fix the Standard of Weights and Measures;

To provide for the Punishment of counterfeiting the Securities and current Coin of the United States;

To establish Post Offices and post Roads;

To promote the Progress of Science and useful Arts, by securing for limited Times to Authors and Inventors the exclusive Right to their respective Writings and Discoveries;

To constitute Tribunals inferior to the supreme Court;

To define and punish Piracies and Felonies committed on the high Seas, and Offences against the Law of Nations;

To declare War, grant Letters of Marque and Reprisal, and make rules concerning Captures on Land and Water;

To raise and support Armies, but no Appropriation of Money to that Use shall be for a longer Term than two Years;

To provide and maintain a Navy;

To make Rules for the Government and Regulation of the Land and naval Forces;

To provide for calling forth the Militia to execute the Laws of the Union, suppress Insurrections and repel Invasions;

To provide for organizing, arming, and disciplining, the Militia, and for governing such Part of them as may be employed in the Service of the United States, reserving to the States respectively, the Appointment of the Officers, and the Authority of training the Militia according to the discipline prescribed by Congress;

To exercise exclusive Legislation in all Cases whatsoever, over such District (not exceeding ten Miles square) as may, by Cession of particular States, and the Acceptance of Congress, become the Seat of the Government of the United States, and to exercise like Authority over all Places purchased by the Consent of the Legislature of the State in which the Same shall be, for the Erection of Forts, Magazines, Arsenals, dock-Yards, and other needful Buildings;—And

To make all Laws which shall be necessary and proper for carrying into Execution the foregoing Powers, and all other Powers vested by this Constitution in the Government of the United States, or in any Department or Officer thereof.

SECTION 9. The Migration or Importation of such Persons as any of the States now existing shall think proper to admit, shall not be prohibited by the Congress prior to the Year one thousand eight hundred and eight, but a tax or duty may be imposed on such Importation, not exceeding ten dollars for each Person.

The Privilege of the Writ of Habeas Corpus shall not be suspended, unless when in Cases of Rebellion or Invasion the public Safety may require it.

No Bill of Attainder or ex post facto Law shall be passed.

No Capitation, or other direct, Tax shall be laid, unless in Proportion to the Census or Enumeration herein before directed to be taken.

No Tax or Duty shall be laid on Articles exported from any State.

No Preference shall be given by any Regulation of Commerce or Revenue to the Ports of one State over those of another: nor shall Vessels bound to, or from, one State, be obliged to enter, clear, or pay Duties in another.

No Money shall be drawn from the Treasury, but in Consequence of Appropriations made by Law; and a regular Statement and Account of the Receipts and Expenditures of all public Money shall be published from time to time.

No Title of Nobility shall be granted by the United States: And no Person holding any Office of Profit or Trust under them, shall, without the consent of the Congress, accept of any present, Emolument, Office, or Title, of any kind whatever, from any King, Prince, or foreign State.

SECTION 10. No State shall enter into any Treaty, Alliance, or Confederation; grant Letters of Marque and Reprisal; coin Money; emit Bills of Credit; make any Thing but gold and silver Coin a Tender in Payment of Debts; pass any Bill of Attainder, ex post facto Law, or Law impairing the Obligation of Contracts, or grant any Title of Nobility.

No State shall, without the Consent of the Congress, lay any Imposts or Duties on Imports or Exports, except what may be absolutely necessary for executing its inspection Laws: and the net Produce of all Duties and Imposts, laid by any State on Imports or Exports, shall be for the Use of the Treasury of the United States; and all such Laws shall be subject to the Revision and Control of the Congress.

No State shall, without the Consent of Congress, lay any Duty of Tonnage, keep Troops, or Ships of War in time of Peace, enter into any Agreement or Compact with another State, or with a foreign Power, or engage in War, unless actually invaded, or in such imminent Danger as will not admit of delay.

Article II

SECTION 1. The executive Power shall be vested in a President of the United States of America. He shall hold his Office during the Term of four Years, and, together with the Vice President, chosen for the same Term, be elected, as follows.

Each State shall appoint, in such Manner as the Legislature thereof may direct, a Number of Electors equal to the whole Number of Senators and Representatives to which the State may be entitled in the Congress: but no Senator or Representative, or Person holding an Office of Trust or Profit under the United States, shall be appointed an Elector.

The Electors shall meet in their respective States, and vote by Ballot for two Persons, of whom one at least shall not be an Inhabitant of the same State with themselves. And they shall make a List of all the Persons voted for, and of the Number of Votes for each; which List they shall sign and certify, and transmit sealed to the Seat of the Government of the United States, directed to the President of the Senate. The President of the Senate shall, in the Presence of the Senate and House of Representatives, open all the Certificates, and the Votes shall then be counted. The Person having the greatest Number of Votes shall be the President, if such Number be a Majority of the whole Number of Electors appointed; and if there be more than one who have such Majority, and have an equal Number of Votes, then the House of Representatives shall immediately chuse by Ballot one of them for President; and if no Person have a Majority, then from the five highest on the List the said House shall in like Manner chuse the President. But in chusing the President, the Votes shall be taken by States, the Representation from each State having one Vote; A quorum for this Purpose shall consist of a Member or Members from two thirds of the States, and a Majority of all the States shall be necessary to a Choice. In every case, after the Choice of the President, the Person having the greatest Number of Votes of the Electors shall be the Vice President. But if there should remain two or more who have equal Votes, the Senate shall chuse from them by Ballot the Vice President.

The Congress may determine the Time of chusing the Electors, and the Day on which they shall give their Votes; which Day shall be the same throughout the United States.

No person except a natural born Citizen, or a Citizen of the United States, at the time of the Adoption of this Constitution, shall be eligible to the Office of President; neither shall any Person be eligible to that Office who shall not have attained to the Age of thirty five Years, and been fourteen Years a Resident within the United States.

In Case of the Removal of the President from Office, or of his Death, Resignation, or Inability to discharge the Powers and Duties of the said Office, the Same shall devolve on the Vice President, and the Congress may by Law provide for the Case of Removal, Death, Resignation or Inability, both of the President and Vice President, declaring what Officer shall then act as President, and such Officer shall act accordingly, until the Disability be removed, or a President shall be elected.

The President shall, at stated Times, receive for his Services, a Compensation, which shall neither be encreased nor diminished during the Period for which he shall have been elected, and he shall not receive within that Period any other Emolument from the United States, or any of them.

Before he enter on the Execution of his Office, he shall take the following Oath or Affirmation:—"I do solemnly swear (or affirm) that I will faithfully execute the Office of President of the United States, and will to the best of my Ability, preserve, protect and defend the Constitution of the United States."

SECTION 2. The President shall be Commander in Chief of the Army and Navy of the United States, and of the Militia of the several States, when called into the actual Service of the United States; he may require the Opinion, in writing, of the principal Officer in each of the executive Departments, upon any Subject relating to the Duties of their respective Offices, and he shall have Power to grant Reprieves and Pardons for Offences against the United States, except in Cases of Impeachment.

He shall have Power, by and with the Advice and Consent of the Senate, to make Treaties, provided two thirds of the Senators present concur; and he shall nominate, and by and with the Advice and Consent of the Senate, shall appoint Ambassadors, other public ministers and Consuls, Judges of the supreme Court, and all other Officers of the United States, whose Appointments are not herein otherwise provided for, and which shall be established by Law: but the Congress may by Law vest the Appointment of such inferior Officers, as they think proper, in the President alone, in the Courts of Law, or in the Heads of Departments.

The President shall have Power to fill up all Vacancies that may happen during the Recess of the Senate, by granting Commissions which shall expire at the End of their next Session.

SECTION 3. He shall from time to time give to the Congress Information of the State of the Union, and recommend to their Consideration such Measures as he shall judge necessary and expedient; he may, on extraordinary Occasions, convene both Houses, or either of them, and in Case of Disagreement between them, with Respect to the Time of Adjournment, he may adjourn them to such Time as he shall think proper; he shall receive Ambassadors and other public Ministers; he shall take Care that the Laws be faithfully executed, and shall Commission all the Officers of the United States.

SECTION 4. The President, Vice President and all civil Officers of the United States, shall be removed from Office on Impeachment for, and Conviction of, Treason, Bribery, or other high Crimes and Misdemeanors.

Article III

SECTION 1. The judicial Power of the United States, shall be vested in one supreme Court, and in such inferior Courts as the Congress may from time to time ordain and establish. The Judges, both of the supreme and inferior Courts, shall hold their Offices during good Behavior, and shall, at stated Times, receive for their Services, a Compensation, which shall not be diminished during their Continuance in Office.

SECTION 2. The judicial Power shall extend to all Cases, in Law and Equity, arising under this Constitution, the Laws of the United States, and Treaties made, or which shall be made, under their Authority;— to all Cases affecting Ambassadors, other public Ministers and Consuls;—to all Cases of admiralty and maritime Jurisdiction;—to Controversies to which the United States shall be a Party;—to Controversies between two or more States;—between a State and Citizens of another State;—between Citizens of different States;—between Citizens of the same State claiming Lands under Grants of different States, and between a State, or the citizens thereof, and foreign States, Citizens or Subjects.

In all Cases affecting Ambassadors, other public Ministers and Consuls, and those in which a State shall be Party, the supreme Court shall have original Jurisdiction. In all the other Cases before mentioned, the supreme Court shall have appellate Jurisdiction, both as to Law and Fact, with such Exceptions, and under such Regulations as the Congress shall make.

The Trial of all Crimes, except in Cases of Impeachment, shall be by Jury; and such Trial shall be held in the State where the said Crimes shall have been committed; but when not committed within any State, the Trial shall be at such Place or Places as the Congress may by Law have directed.

SECTION 3. Treason against the United States, shall consist only in levying War against them, or in adhering to their Enemies, giving them Aid and Comfort. No Person shall be convicted of Treason unless on the Testimony of two Witnesses to the same overt Act, or on Confession in open Court.

The Congress shall have Power to declare the Punishment of Treason, but no Attainder of Treason shall work Corruption of Blood, or Forfeiture except during the Life of the Person attainted.

Article IV

SECTION 1. Full Faith and Credit shall be given in each State to the public Acts, Records, and judicial Proceedings of every other State. And the Congress may by general Laws prescribe the Manner in which such Acts, Records and Proceedings shall be proved, and the Effect thereof.

SECTION 2. The Citizens of each State shall be entitled to Privileges and Immunities of Citizens in the several States.

A Person charged in any State with Treason, Felony, or other Crime, who shall flee from Justice, and be found in another State, shall on Demand of the executive Authority of the State from which he fled, be delivered up, to be removed to the State having Jurisdiction of the Crime.

No Person held to Service or Labour in one State, under the Laws thereof, escaping into another, shall, in Consequence of any Law or Regulation therein, be discharged from such Service or Labour, but shall be delivered up on Claim of the Party to whom such Service or Labour may be due.

SECTION 3. New States may be admitted by the Congress into this Union; but no new State shall be formed or erected within the Jurisdiction of any other State; nor any State be formed by the Junction of two or more States, or Parts of States, without the Consent of the Legislatures of the States concerned as well as of the Congress.

The Congress shall have Power to dispose of and make all needful Rules and Regulations respecting the Territory or other Property belonging to the United States; and nothing in this Constitution shall be so construed as to Prejudice any Claims of the United States, or of any particular State.

SECTION 4. The United States shall guarantee to every State in this Union a Republican Form of Government, and shall protect each of them against

Invasion; and on Application of the Legislature, or of the Executive (when the Legislature cannot be convened) against domestic Violence.

Article V
The Congress, whenever two thirds of both Houses shall deem it necessary, shall propose Amendments to this Constitution, or, on the Application of the Legislatures of two thirds of the several States, shall call a Convention for proposing Amendments, which, in either Case, shall be valid to all Intents and Purposes, as Part of this Constitution, when ratified by the Legislatures of three fourths of the several States, or by Conventions in three fourths thereof, as the one or the other Mode of Ratification may be proposed by the Congress; Provided that no Amendment which may be made prior to the Year One thousand eight hundred and eight shall in any Manner affect the first and fourth Clauses in the Ninth Section of the first Article; and that no State, without its Consent, shall be deprived of its equal Suffrage in the Senate.

Article VI
All Debts contracted and Engagements entered into, before the Adoption of this Constitution, shall be as valid against the United States under this Constitution, as under the Confederation.

This Constitution, and the Laws of the United States which shall be made in Pursuance thereof; and all Treaties made, or which shall be made, under the Authority of the United States, shall be the supreme Law of the Land; and the Judges in every State shall be bound thereby, any Thing in the Constitution or Laws of any State to the contrary notwithstanding.

The Senators and Representatives before mentioned, and the Members of the several State Legislatures, and all executive and judicial Officers, both of the United States and of the several States, shall be bound by Oath or Affirmation, to support this Constitution; but no religious Test shall ever be required as a Qualification to any Office or public Trust under the United States.

Article VII
The Ratification of the Conventions of nine States, shall be sufficient for the Establishment of this Constitution between the States so ratifying the Same.

Done in Convention by the Unanimous Consent of the States present the Seventeenth Day of September in the Year of our Lord one thousand seven hundred and Eighty seven and of the Independence of the United States of America the Twelfth. In witness whereof We have hereunto subscribed our Names.

The Bill of Rights

(Ratification of the first ten amendments was completed on December 15, 1791)

Amendment I

Congress shall make no law respecting an establishment of religion, or prohibiting the free exercise thereof; or abridging the freedom of speech, or of the press; or the right of the people peaceably to assemble, and to petition the Government for a redress of grievances.

Amendment II

A well regulated Militia, being necessary to the security of a free State, the right of the people to keep and bear Arms, shall not be infringed.

Amendment III

No Soldier shall, in time of peace be quartered in any house, without the consent of the Owner, nor in time of war, but in a manner to be prescribed by law.

Amendment IV

The right of the people to be secure in their persons, houses, papers, and effects, against unreasonable searches and seizures, shall not be violated, and no Warrants shall issue, but upon probable cause, supported by Oath or affirmation, and particularly describing the place to be searched, and the persons or things to be seized.

Amendment V

No person shall be held to answer for a capital, or otherwise infamous crime, unless on a presentment or indictment of a Grand Jury, except in cases arising in the land or naval forces, or in the Militia, when in actual service in time of War or public danger; nor shall any person be subject for the same offence to be twice put in jeopardy of life or limb; nor shall be compelled in any criminal case to be a witness against himself, nor be deprived of life, liberty, or property, without due process of law; nor shall private property be taken for public use, without just compensation.

Amendment VI

In all criminal prosecutions, the accused shall enjoy the right to a speedy and public trial, by an impartial jury of the State and district wherein the crime shall have been committed, which district shall have been previously ascertained by law, and to be informed of the nature and cause of the accusation; to be confronted with the witnesses against him; to have compulsory process for obtaining witnesses in his favor, and to have the Assistance of Counsel for his defence.

Amendment VII

In Suits at common law, where the value in controversy shall exceed twenty dollars, the right of trial by jury shall be preserved, and no fact tried by a jury, shall be otherwise re-examined in any Court of the United States, than according to the rules of the common law.

Amendment VIII

Excessive bail shall not be required, nor excessive fines imposed, nor cruel and unusual punishments inflicted.

Amendment IX

The enumeration in the Constitution, of certain rights, shall not be construed to deny or disparage others retained by the people.

Amendment X

The powers not delegated to the United States by the Constitution, nor prohibited by it to the States, are reserved to the States respectively, or to the people.

Amendment XI
January 8, 1798

The Judicial power of the United States shall not be construed to extend to any suit in law or equity, commenced or prosecuted against one of the United States by Citizens of another State, or by Citizens or Subjects of any Foreign State.

Amendment XII
September 25, 1804

The Electors shall meet in their respective states, and vote by ballot for President and Vice President, one of whom, at least, shall not be an inhabitant of the same state with themselves; they shall name in their ballots the person voted for as President, and in distinct ballots the person voted for as Vice President, and they shall make distinct lists of all persons voted for as President, and of all persons voted for as Vice President, and of the number of votes for each, which lists they shall sign and certify and transmit sealed to the seat of the government of the United States, directed to the President of the Senate;—The President of the Senate shall, in the presence of the Senate and House of Representatives, open all the certificates and the votes shall then be counted;—The person having the greatest number of votes for President, shall be the President, if such number be a majority of the whole number of Electors appointed; and if no person have such majority, then from the persons having the highest numbers not exceeding three on the list of those voted for as President, the House of Representatives shall choose immediately, by ballot, the President. But in choosing the President, the votes shall be taken by states, the representation from each State having one vote; a quorum for this purpose shall consist of a member or members from two-thirds of the states, and a majority of all the states shall be necessary to a choice. And if the House of Representatives shall not choose a President whenever the right of choice shall devolve upon them, before the fourth day of March next following, then the Vice President shall act as President, as in the case of the death or other constitutional disability of the President. — The person having the greatest number of votes as Vice President, shall be the Vice President, if such number be a majority of the whole number of Electors appointed, and if no person have a majority, then from the two highest numbers on the list, the Senate shall choose the Vice President; a quorum for the purpose shall consist of two-thirds of the whole number of Senators, and a majority of the whole number shall be necessary to a choice. But no person constitutionally ineligible to the office of President shall be eligible to that of Vice President of the United States.

Amendment XII
December 18, 1865
SECTION 1. Neither slavery nor involuntary servitude, except as a punishment for crime whereof the party shall have been duly convicted, shall exist within the United States, or any place subject to their jurisdiction.

SECTION 2. Congress shall have power to enforce this article by appropriate legislation.

Amendment XIV
July 9, 1868

SECTION 1. All persons born or naturalized in the United States, and subject to the jurisdiction thereof, are citizens of the United States and of the State wherein they reside. No State shall make or enforce any law which shall abridge the privileges or immunities of citizens of the United States; nor shall any State deprive any person of life, liberty, or property, without due process of law; nor deny to any person within its jurisdiction the equal protection of the laws.

SECTION 2. Representatives shall be apportioned among the several States according to their respective numbers, counting the whole number of persons in each State, excluding Indians not taxed. But when the right to vote at any election for the choice of electors for President and Vice President of the United States, Representatives in Congress, the Executive and Judicial officers of a State, or the members of the Legislature thereof, is denied to any of the male inhabitants of such State, being twenty-one years of age, and citizens of the United States, or in any way abridged, except for participation in rebellion, or other crime, the basis of representation therein shall be reduced in the proportion which the number of such male citizens shall bear to the whole number of male citizens twenty-one years of age in such State.

SECTION 3. No person shall be a Senator or Representative in Congress, or elector of President and Vice President, or hold any office, civil or military, under the United States, or under any State, who, having previously taken an oath, as a member of Congress, or as an officer of the United States, or as a member of any State legislature, or as an executive or judicial officer of any State, to support the Constitution of the United States, shall have engaged in insurrection or rebellion against the same, or given aid or comfort to the enemies thereof. But Congress may by a vote of two-thirds of each House, remove such disability.

SECTION 4. The validity of the public debt of the United States, authorized by law, including debts incurred for payment of pensions and bounties for services in suppressing insurrection or rebellion, shall not be questioned. But neither the United States nor any State shall assume or pay any debt or obligation incurred in aid of insurrection or rebellion against the United States, or any claim for the loss or emancipation of any slave; but all such debts, obligations and claims shall be held illegal and void.

SECTION 5. The Congress shall have power to enforce, by appropriate legislation, the provisions of this article.

Appendix C

Amendment XV
March 30, 1870
SECTION 1. The right of citizens of the United States to vote shall not be denied or abridged by the United States or by any State on account of race, color, or previous conditions of servitude.

SECTION 2. The Congress shall have power to enforce this article by appropriate legislation.

Amendment XVI
February 25, 1913
The Congress shall have power to lay and collect taxes on incomes, from whatever source derived, without apportionment among the several States, and without regard to any census or enumeration.

Amendment XVII
May 31, 1913
The Senate of the United States shall be composed of two Senators from each State, elected by the people thereof, for six years; and each Senator shall have one vote. The electors in each State shall have the qualifications requisite for electors of the most numerous branch of the State legislatures.

When vacancies happen in the representation of any State in the Senate, the executive authority of such State shall issue writs of election to fill such vacancies: *Provided*, That the legislature of any State may empower the executive thereof to make temporary appointments until the people fill the vacancies by election as the legislature may direct.

This amendment shall not be so construed as to affect the election or term of any Senator chosen before it becomes valid as part of the Constitution.

Amendment XVIII
January 29, 1919
SECTION 1. After one year from the ratification of this article, the manufacture, sale, or transportation of intoxicating liquors within, the importation thereof into, or the exportation thereof from the United States and all territory subject to the jurisdiction thereof for beverage purposes is hereby prohibited.

SECTION 2. The Congress and the several States shall have concurrent power to enforce this article by appropriate legislation.

SECTION 3. This Article shall be inoperative unless it shall have been ratified as an amendment to the Constitution by the legislatures of the several States, as provided in the Constitution, within seven years from the date of the submission hereof to the States by the Congress.

Amendment XIX
January 26, 1920

The right of citizens of the United States to vote shall not be denied or abridged by the United States or by any State on account of sex.

Congress shall have power to enforce this article by appropriate legislation.

Amendment XX
February 6, 1933

SECTION 1. The terms of the President and Vice President shall end at noon on the 20th day of January, and the terms of Senators and Representatives at noon on the 3d day of January, of the years in which such terms would have ended if this article had not been ratified; and the terms of their successors shall then begin.

SECTION 2. The Congress shall assemble at least once in every year, and such meeting shall begin at noon on the 3d day of January, unless they shall by law appoint a different day.

SECTION 3. If, at the time fixed for the beginning of the term of the President, the President elect shall have died, the Vice President elect shall become President. If a President shall not have been chosen before the time fixed for the beginning of his term, or if the President elect shall have failed to qualify, then the Vice President elect shall act as President until a President shall have qualified; and the Congress may by law provide for the case wherein neither a President elect nor a Vice President elect shall have qualified, declaring who shall then act as President, or the manner in which one who is to act shall be selected, and such person shall act accordingly until a President or Vice President shall have qualified.

SECTION 4. The Congress may by law provide for the case of the death of any of the persons from whom the House of Representatives may choose a President whenever the right of choice shall have devolved upon them, and for the case of the death of any of the persons from whom the Senate may choose a Vice President whenever the right of choice shall have devolved upon them.

SECTION 5. Sections 1 and 2 shall take effect on the 15th day of October following the ratification of this article.

SECTION 6. This article shall be inoperative unless it shall have been ratified as an amendment to the Constitution by the legislatures of three-fourths of the several States within seven years from the date of its submission.

Amendment XXI
December 5, 1933

SECTION 1. The eighteenth article of amendment to the Constitution of the United States is hereby repealed.

SECTION 2. The transportation or importation into any State, Territory, or possession of the United States for delivery or use therein of intoxicating liquors, in violation of the laws thereof, is hereby prohibited.

SECTION 3. The article shall be inoperative unless it shall have been ratified as an amendment to the Constitution by conventions in the several States, as provided in the Constitution, within seven years from the date of the submission hereof to the States by the Congress.

Amendment XXII
February 27, 1951

SECTION 1. No person shall be elected to the office of the President more than twice, and no person who has held the office of President, or acted as President, for more than two years of a term to which some other person was elected President shall be elected to the office of the President more than once. But this article shall not apply to any person holding the office of President when this article was proposed by the Congress, and shall not prevent any person who may be holding the office of President, or acting as President, during the term within which this article becomes operative from holding the office of President or acting as President during the remainder of such term.

SECTION 2. This article shall be inoperative unless it shall have been ratified as an amendment to the Constitution by the legislatures of three-fourths of the several States within seven years from the date of its submission to the States by the Congress.

Amendment XXIII
March 29, 1961

SECTION 1. The District constituting the seat of Government of the United States shall appoint in such manner as the Congress may direct:

A number of electors of President and Vice President equal to the whole number of Senators and Representatives in Congress to which the District would be entitled if it were a State, but in no event more than the least populous State; they shall be in addition to those appointed by the States, but they shall be considered, for the purposes of the election of President and Vice President, to be electors appointed by a State; and they shall meet in the District and perform such duties as provided by the twelfth article of amendment.

SECTION 2. The Congress shall have power to enforce this article by appropriate legislation.

Amendment XXIV
January 24, 1964

SECTION 1. The right of citizens of the United States to vote in any primary or other election for President or Vice President, for electors for President or Vice President, or for Senator or Representative in Congress, shall not be denied or abridged by the United States or any State by reason of failure to pay any poll tax or other tax.

SECTION 2. The Congress shall have power to enforce this article by appropriate legislation.

Amendment XXV
February 10, 1967

SECTION 1. In case of the removal of the President from office or his death or resignation, the Vice President shall become President.

SECTION 2. Whenever there is a vacancy in the office of the Vice President, the President shall nominate a Vice President who shall take the office upon confirmation by a majority vote of both houses of Congress.

SECTION 3. Whenever the President transmits to the President pro tempore of the Senate and the Speaker of the House of Representatives his written declaration that he is unable to discharge the powers and duties of his office, and until he transmits to them a written declaration to the contrary, such powers and duties shall be discharged by the Vice President as Acting President.

SECTION 4. Whenever the Vice President and a majority of either the principal officers of the executive departments, or of such other body as Congress may by law provide, transmit to the President pro tempore of the Senate and the Speaker of the House of Representatives their written declaration that the President is unable to discharge the powers and duties of his office, the Vice President shall immediately assume the powers and duties of the office as Acting President.

Thereafter, when the President transmits to the President pro tempore of the Senate and the Speaker of the House of Representatives his written declaration that no inability exists, he shall resume the powers and duties of his office unless the Vice President and a majority of either the principal officers of the executive department or of such other body as Congress may by law provide, transmit within four days to the President pro tempore of the Senate and the Speaker of the House of Representatives their written declaration that the President is unable to discharge the powers and duties of his office. Thereupon Congress shall decide the issue, assembling within 48 hours for that purpose if not in session. If the Congress, within 21 days after receipt of the latter written declaration, or, if Congress is not in session, within 21 days after Congress is required to assemble, determines by two thirds vote of both houses that the President is unable to discharge the powers and duties of his office, the Vice President shall continue to discharge the same as Acting President; otherwise, the President shall resume the powers and duties of his office.

Amendment XXVI
June 30, 1971
SECTION 1. The right of citizens of the United States, who are eighteen years of age or older, to vote shall not be denied or abridged by the United States or by any State on account of age.

SECTION 2. The Congress shall have power to enforce this article by appropriate legislation.

Amendment XXVII
May 7, 1992
No law, varying the compensation for the services of the Senators and Representatives, shall take effect, until an election of Representatives shall have intervened.

SUGGESTED READING

Aquinas, St. Thomas. *Truth*. Chicago: Henry Regnery Company, 1954.

Aristotle. *Basic Works of Aristotle*. Edited by Richard Peter McKeon. New York: Random House, 1941.

Armey, Dick. *The Freedom Revolution*. Chicago: Henry Regnery Company, 1995.

Bastiat, Frederic. *The Law*. Translated by Dean Russell. Irvington-on-Hudson, N.Y.: Foundation for Economic Education, 1981.

Bennett, William. *The Book of Virtues*. New York: Simon & Schuster, 1995.

Bigongiari, Dina. *The Political Ideas of St. Thomas Aquinas*. New York: Hafner Publishing, Inc., 1953.

Bovard, James. *Lost Rights*. New York: St. Martin's Press, 1992.

Buckley, William F., Jr. *Up from Liberalism*. New York: Hillman Periodicals, Inc., 1959.

Budget of the United States Government—1993. Washington, D.C.: U.S. Government Printing Office, 1994.

Carson, Clarence B. *The Fateful Turn*. Irvington-on-Hudson, N.Y.: Foundation for Economic Education, 1963.

Catlin, George. *The Story of Political Philosophers*. New York: McGraw-Hill Book Company, 1939.

Chamberlain, William Henry. *The Evolution of a Conservative*. Chicago: Henry Regnery Company, 1959.

Cobban, Alfred. *Edmund Burke and the Revolt Against the 18th Century*. New York: Macmillan Company, 1961.

Coker, Francis William. *Readings in Political Philosophy*. New York: Macmillan Company, 1938.

Crane, Philip M. *The Democrat's Dilemma*. Chicago: Henry Regnery Company, 1964.

———. *The Sum of Good Government*. Ottawa, Ill.: Green Hill Publishers, Inc. 1976.

Davenport, John. *The U.S. Economy*. Chicago: Henry Regnery Company, 1964.

Dos Passos, John. *Occasions and Protests*. Chicago: Henry Regnery Company, 1964.

Dunning, William A. *A History of Political Theories*. New York: Macmillan Company, 1905.

Emerson, Ralph Waldo. *Essays*. New York: Crowell Company, 1926.

Essays on Liberty. Irvington-on-Hudson, N.Y.: Foundation for Economic Education, 1952–1976.

Suggested Reading

The Essential Left: Marx, Engels, Lenin. New York: Barnes & Noble, 1961.

Evans, M. Stanton. *Clear and Present Dangers.* New York: Harcourt, Brace, Jovanovich, 1976.

————. *The Fringe on Top.* New York: American Features, 1963.

————. *The Liberal Establishment.* New York: Devin-Adair Company, 1965.

————. *The Revolt on Campus.* Chicago: Henry Regnery Company, 1961.

The Federalist Papers. Edited by Clinton Rossiter. New York: New American Library, 1961.

Fertig, Lawrence. *Prosperity Through Freedom.* Chicago: Henry Regnery Company, 1961.

Figgie, Harry, Jr. *Bankruptcy 1995.* Boston: Little, Brown, 1992.

Frederich, Carl J. *The Philosophy of Hegel.* New York: Holt, Rinehart & Winston, 1962.

Gibbon, Edward. *The Decline and Fall of the Roman Empire.* 3 volumes. New York: Modern Library, 1937.

Gingrich, Newt. *To Renew America.* New York: HarperCollins, 1995.

Goldwater, Barry M. *The Conscience of a Conservative.* Shepherdsville, Ky.: Victor Publishing Co., 1960.

Gross, Martin. *A Call for Revolution.* New York: Ballantine, 1995.

————. *Government Racket: Washington Waste from A to Z.* New York: Bantam, 1992).

Harman, J. Judd. *Political Thought from Plato to the Present.* New York: McGraw-Hill Book Company, 1946.

Harvey, Paul M. *Autumn of Liberty.* New York: Hanover House, 1954.

————. *Remember These Things.* Chicago: Heritage Press, 1952.

————. *The Rest of the Story.* Chicago: Hanover House, 1952.

Hayek, Friedrich A. von. *The Road to Serfdom.* Chicago: University of Chicago Press, 1944.

Hazlitt, Henry. *Economics in One Lesson.* New York: Harper & Brothers, 1946

Hume, David. *An Enquiry Concerning Human Understanding.* Chicago: Henry Regnery Company, 1956.

Jones, Robert V. *The Challenge of Liberty.* Chicago: Heritage Press, 1956.

Kennedy, William. *The Grace Commission Report.* Ottawa, Ill.: Green Hill Publishers, 1984.

Kirk, Russell. *The Conservative Mind.* Chicago: Henry Regnery Company, 1953.

Lambro, Donald. *The Federal Rathole.* New Rochelle, N.Y.: Arlington House, 1975.

Locke, John. *Essays Concerning Human Understanding.* Chicago: Henry Regnery Company, 1956.

———. *A Letter Concerning Toleration.* New York: Macmillan Company, 1956.

———. *Second Treatise on Government.* New York: Macmillan Company, 1956.

Machiavelli, Niccolò, *The Prince* and *The Discourses.* New York: Modern Library, 1950.

Marx, Karl. *Capital.* New York: Modern Library, 1906.

———, and Friedrich Engels. *The Communist Manifesto.* Chicago: Henry Regnery Company, 1961.

McDonald, Forrest. *The American Presidency.* Lawrence: University of Kansas Press, 1994.

McGovern, William M. *Strategic Intelligence and the Shape of Tomorrow.* Chicago: Henry Regnery Company, 1961.

McIlwain, Charles H. *The Growth of Political Thought in the West.* New York: Macmillan, 1932.

McLean, Edward B., ed. *Derailing the Constitution.*Wilmington, Del.: Intercollegiate Studies Institute, 1995.

Meigs, William. *The Growth of the Constitution.* New York: J. E. Lippincott, 1900.

Meyer, Alfred G. *Marxism: The Unity of Theory and Practice.* Cambridge: Harvard University Press, 1954.

Mill, John Stuart. *Essential Works.* Edited by Max Lerner. New York: Bantam, 1995.

———. *On Liberty.* Chicago: Henry Regnery Company, 1956.

von Mises, Ludwig. *Human Action.* New Haven, Conn.: Yale University Press, 1949.

———. *Omnipotent Government.* New Haven, Conn.: Yale University Press, 1949.

Montesquieu, Charles de. *The Spirit of Laws.* New York: Hafner Publishing Co., 1949.

Nash, George H. *The Conservative Intellectual Movement in America.* New York: Basic Books, 1976.

Plato. *The Republic.* Translated by A. D. Lindsay. New York: E. P. Dutton & Co., 1949.

Rafferty, Max. *Suffer, Little Children.* New York: Devin-Adair Company, 1982.

Read, Leonard E. *Elements of Libertarian Leadership.* Irvington-on-Hudson, N.Y.: Foundation for Economic Education, 1965.

———. *The Free Market and Its Enemy.* Irvington-on-Hudson, N.Y.: Foundation for Economic Education, 1965.

————. *Why Not Try Freedom?* Irvington-on-Hudson, N.Y.: Foundation for Economic Education, 1965.

Richberg, Donald R. *Labor Union Monopoly.* Chicago: Henry Regnery Company, 1957.

Roepke, Wilhelm. *Economics of the Free Society.* Chicago: Henry Regnery Company, 1963.

Rousseau, Jean Jacques. *The Social Contact* and *The Discourses.* New York: E. P. Dutton Co., 1913.

Rudd, Augustin. *Bending of the Twig.* Chicago: Heritage Press, 1957.

Smith, Adam. *The Wealth of Nations.* New York: Modern Library, 1928.

Sowell, Thomas. *The Vision of the Anointed.* New York: Basic Books, 1995.

Stanlis, Peter J. *Edmund Burke and the Natural Law.* Ann Arbor: University of Michigan Press, 1958.

Statistical Abstract of the United State,1993. Washington, D.C.: U.S. Government Printing Office, 1994.

Tocqueville, Alexis de. *Democracy in America.* 2 volumes. New York: Oxford University Press, 1952.

Voegelin, Eric. *Plato and Aristotle: Order and History.* Baton Rouge: Louisiana State University, 1957.

Weaver, Henry Grady. *The Mainspring of Human Progress.* Irvington-on-Hudson, N.Y.: Foundation for Economic Education, 1953.

Weaver, Richard M. *Ideas Have Consequences.* Chicago: University of Chicago Press, 1948.

Weyl, Nathaniel, and Stefan Possony. *The Geography of Intellect.* Chicago: Henry Regnery Company, 1963.

Will, George. *The Leveling Wind.* New York: Viking Press, 1994.

Wolfe, Gregory. *A New Dawn of Liberty.* Century City, Ca.: Salvatori, 1992.

Wolin, Sheldon S. *Politics and Vision.* Boston: Little, Brown, 1960.

Wormuth, Francis L. *The Origins of Modern Constitutionalism.* New York: Harper & Row, 1949.

JAMES R. EVANS is an author, lecturer, historian, and retired business executive.

He is a graduate of the University of Michigan and a past president of the American Machine Tool Distributors Association.

He is a veteran of World War II, having served as an officer with the Thirteenth Air Force in the South Pacific Theater.

Over forty years ago, Mr. Evans embarked on a course of study involving several hundred volumes covering theology, history, economics, philosophy, and political science. A number of these are listed in the selected readings contained within this volume.

These inquiries culminated in more than a hundred lectures and two previous books: *The Glorious Quest—Reflections on American Political Philosophy* (Chicago: Charles Hallberg & Company, 1967) and *America's Choice—Twilight's Last Gleaming or Dawn's Early Light?* (Dallas, Tex.: Fisher/Caroline, 1981).

Mr. Evans serves on the board of trustees of both the Intercollegiate Studies Institute and the Philadelphia Society.

He, his wife Dori, and their golden retriever Marigold reside in Indian Wells, California.